"So wisely and tenderly v
Rabbi Barclay uncovers o
align with the spiritual la
inner work required to profoundly interface with the Divine and
one another."

— Michael Bernard Beckwith, author of *Life Visioning*

"Rabbi Barclay's book is a reminder of the golden threads which join
so many different religions. This is particularly true of the Jewish and
Christian faiths which share history and a sacred literature. This book
will give spiritual comfort to many grateful readers."

— Christopher (Lord) Patten
Chancellor of the University of Oxford

"The books in the third section of the Bible are often inaccessible to
people. Rabbi Barclay is a sure guide to the understanding of the text,
but even more, he opens the door to insightful application of these
sacred treasures to the life of the reader. To go with him, his book and
Bible in hand, is a wonderful spiritual adventure."

— Rabbi Zalman Schachter-Shalomi, author of *Davening*

"Michael Barclay brings to this study of the Ketuvim the unique
perspective of a Jewish rabbi who has taught in a Catholic university.
He does a masterful job of blending scholarship and spirituality. His
controlling insight that these biblical books show us how to
'experience God in every relationship' makes this book a valuable tool
for learning how to live well."

— Irene Nowell, OSB
Benedictine of Mount St. Scholastica and adjunct
professor of Scripture at Saint John's School of
Theology•Seminary, Collegeville, Minnesota

Sacred Relationships

Biblical Wisdom for
Deepening Our Lives Together

To yoCHAEVED

Rabbi Michael Barclay

FOR MY BELOVED FRIEND & TEACHER

בברכה   pidea

LITURGICAL PRESS
Collegeville, Minnesota

www.litpress.org

1	2	3	4	5	6	7	8	9

Library of Congress Cataloging-in-Publication Data

Barclay, Michael Lawrence.
    Sacred relationships : biblical wisdom for deepening our lives together / Rabbi Michael Barclay.
      pages cm.
    ISBN 978-0-8146-3518-6 — ISBN 978-0-8146-3543-8 (ebook)
      1. Bible. O.T. Hagiographa—Criticism, interpretation, etc.   I. Title.

BS1308.B37   2013
221.6—dc23
                                        2012042376

Contents

With Gratitude

A person's work is based on the many experiences and people that have affected him, and this book is no exception. I could not have even started working on this without the help, guidance, and support of so many people. If the reader finds any value in this writing, then it is because of my teachers, family, and friends; and before embarking on this journey through the text together, it is important to give the respect due to those who have prepared the trail for us.

As a young man, I often thought about attending rabbinical school, but it was only when the Academy for Jewish Religion, California (AJRCA), opened its pluralistic doors that it became a reality. I did not ever wish to be educated in just one "movement" of Judaism, and I've always believed that one of the weaknesses of our tradition as it is practiced here in America is that we are so divisive among ourselves. It did not matter to Hitler whether someone was a secular, Reform, Conservative, or Orthodox Jew; and it won't matter to the Messiah, may he or she come in our time. So why do we place such emphasis on judging one another? The holy texts of our tradition were given to us all, and AJRCA encouraged, through its diverse faculty and spirit of inclusion, an environment that fostered the creativity and love for text that I now find such an important part of my life. Without the learning and intellectual support that I found there, I could not have even started to analyze text in a creative way.

The people from AJRCA that affected me, both students and faculty, are too many to list here. But it would be inappropriate if

I did not give the honor to some of the teachers who so deeply influenced me, helping my love for our traditions and text grow and flourish. Rabbi Mel Gottlieb, the president of AJRCA, is a greater rabbi than I could ever hope to be. He combines his knowledge and decades of experience with compassion and caring. Dr. Tamar Frankiel, the dean of Academic Affairs, is a truly righteous woman, with an unparalleled understanding of the necessity of combining academics with tradition. Rabbi Steve Robbins has been a lifelong teacher and a tremendous bridge in integrating our mystical tradition with psycho-emotional understandings; and Rabbi Mordecai Finley has been a source of support and strength, and a model for me not only as a rabbi but also as a man. I am grateful to Dr. Joel Gereboff, Dr. Marvin Sweeney, and Dr. Gil Graff for opening my mind to the academic approaches to text; and I am equally grateful to Dr. Vered Hopenstad and Cantor Nate Lam, who live with a passion that exemplifies the very best of our tradition. Rabbis Daniel Bouskila and Haim Ovadia continue to be guides for me to understand the Sephardic approaches to our tradition; and there are no words to describe the blessings I have received from Rabbi Shlomo "Schwartzie" Schwartz, who has constantly pushed me to know the beauty of Hasidism. The combining of joy and depth that I have always experienced from Rabbi Stan Levy and Rabbi J. B. Sacks is a practice that I continue to try to model in all aspects of the teaching that I do.

There are a few men in particular for whom I am more grateful than can be expressed. Ronnie Serr is one of the most knowledgeable and compassionate men I have ever known in my life, and is the embodiment of a tzaddik, a righteous man. Rabbi Avraham Greenbaum of the Azamra Institute in Jerusalem has been an anchor and teacher for my entire family for many years; his teachings, words, and actions have guided me into a level of love for Torah that I never would have imagined decades ago. Rabbi David Baron of The Temple of the Arts has been not only a dear friend but also a wonderful mentor and teacher in integrating the depths of our teachings with the arts of the twenty-first century; and Rabbi Gershon Weissman is a consistent teacher in the art of wisdom through gentleness. Rabbi Shimon Kraft of the 613 Mitzvah Store in Los Angeles is a true teacher of Torah, and has always been an amazing resource for me in all my studies; and Rabbi Aaron Katz is a true master at integrating text into practical applications in the twenty-first century.

Certain people so deeply affect your life in all ways that you do not even know how to begin to define the relationship. I have been blessed to have two of those men not only be friends and teachers but also to act as the witnesses on my *ketubah*, my marriage contract. Rabbi Elijah Schochet is a great scholar and rabbi, a model of what a human being can achieve. As a mutual friend once said of him, "only pearls fall from his mouth," and I was blessed to have him at AJRCA not only as a professor but also as my thesis advisor. I am even more blessed that he continues to be a teacher and friend to my family and me; without his guidance I would never have had the ability, nor even the desire, to find the love of Talmud and our texts that is now so ingrained in my soul. This book is a direct result of his encouragement at all times to learn the text as deeply and personally as possible, and I cannot imagine a better guide into the world of our holy writings. He personifies doing more than is ever required through the way that he walks with beauty, grace, and dignity in the world. Rabbi Arthur Gross Schaefer has been and continues to be my friend and confidant, a guide and support that began long before I embarked on a serious journey into Judaism and continues today. Because of him, I had the opportunity to teach at the university level, which spawned so many of the teachings of this book. He and his family—his son Elisha has even stood by my side as a cantor for multiple High Holiday services—are not only dear friends but also part of that integral support system that every human being so needs.

It is often said that when the student is ready, the teacher appears, and I learned a great deal about what a rabbi can be from a man who was not even Jewish. Anselmo Valencia, of blessed memory, taught me about life, God, the spirit, and community without ever standing in front of me in a classroom. This great man, who was the chief of the Yaqui Indians, would constantly toss out little comments that would cause me to rethink my entire perspective of Life and God, and was one of the great leaders of his people in their history. His family and culture are all a special part of my life, and their friendship is a continued source of caring and strength.

The entire concept for this book came from the many experiences I had while teaching theology at Loyola Marymount University, and I have no doubt that I learned more from the students of my classes than they ever learned from me. Similarly, I learned so much about relationships through spending time with couples at whose weddings I've been blessed to officiate. Experiencing Divinity within the context of a wedding is transforming, and out of all the amazing weddings I have been privileged to be part of, I am especially grateful to Cami and Scott, Dana and Phil, Sonia and Nick, Nicole and Ophir, Anna and Eli, Nicole and Josh, Jessica and David, Judy and Dan, and Coco and Bruce for allowing me to participate in their special days while I was working on this manuscript. Without my friend and teacher Ayodele Adeyemi, I would never have understood and experienced so many of the teachings about passion, joy, and strength that are found in the texts that are explored in this book. Both Ayo and my dear friend Yuval Ron have always been masters and guides for me in integrating the power of music with the presence of God. Like many teenagers, my love for Judaism was enhanced and nurtured through the summer camp experience, and I will always be grateful for the guidance I and so many other young people were given by Stephen Breuer and Chuck Feldman. Ira Boren has modeled living in a sacred way in the workplace; and on the most basic of levels this book would not be here without the hard work of Trish, Andy, Stephanie, and all the wonderful people at Liturgical Press. I am also so grateful to the many periodicals, and especially the *Jewish Journal* of Los Angeles, for allowing me to write and share my thoughts about our tradition in a public setting.

There are those who are no longer with us physically but without whom I would simply not know how to be a man, let alone a rabbi. My brother of blessed memory, John Barclay, Yonaton ben

Avram HaCohen, was my best friend, teacher, and guide; he taught me that every moment and action can be a prayer. My beloved grandmother, Rose Handler, Shoshanah bat Israel, may her memory be a blessing, instilled within me a love and respect for Jewish values, and I know her love is always with me and my family. My parents of blessed memory, George and Iris Barclay, Avram HaCohen and Sara bat Moshe v'Shoshanah, brought me into this world, raised me to have a love and appreciation for life, ethics, Judaism, and to see God in everything and everywhere. They are the roots of my Tree of Life, and I pray that their souls find joy in these writings.

There are teachers and friends, sages and rabbis, but the greatest teachers for me are the ones that I am blessed to be with every day, *B"H*: my wife, Allison, and my sons, Benjamin and Jonathan. They have put up with me while I've been working on this book, guiding me with their thoughts and insights about life—sometimes through words, and often (especially in the case of my toddler twins) through their actions. They remind me of the deep purpose of our lives and are not only my support but also are my teachers in every moment about what is really important in life.

The most thanks and honor must be given to the Creator of All, who has blessed me with life, teachers, and my beloved wife and sons. This entire book is for You, so that all of us may deepen our own relationships with You, and let You into our daily lives.

To each of you, and to so many others . . . my thanks and gratitude for all that you have given me is overwhelming.

May I live in a way that is deserving of your gifts and that brings you joy.

B'shalom u'vracha
Rabbi Michael Barclay

Introduction:
Ketuvim, Biblical Wisdom for Relationships

When we open up a Jewish Bible (called Tanakh, a Hebrew acronym for Torah, Neviʾim, and Ketuvim), we find a beautiful collection of writings that is often called the Ketuvim (meaning "Writings").[1] Included in this section are books of praise and wisdom, pain and suffering, and the entire gamut of human emotions. These books are often considered the "Wisdom literature" of the Bible. Many people from all faith traditions are familiar with the Psalms, which are used so often by all Western religions in rites of passage and life-cycle rituals; with the book of Proverbs, which gives practical advice on how to live and love; and with Job, which is the archetype used by everyone from clergy to psychologists to understand the ancient question of "why bad things happen to good people." These, and the other books of this section of Scripture, are quoted and used by people from all walks of life. But is there possibly a deeper meaning hidden in all of these books that ties them together? How can we use these powerful texts to enhance our own lives and our relationship with God? Are there commonalities between these texts that can help us live more passionately, fully, and consciously? Simply put, what are these books really all about?

To understand the Ketuvim, we need to look at all the books individually, as well as their history and placement, and examine any potential ties that bind them together thematically. We need to become "Bible detectives"—questioning and turning over the texts to understand and integrate them at a deep and full level.

1

As we do this, we may find that there is much more to Psalms than just comforting us in our grief, more to Job than just a question about suffering, and a hidden depth to each of these books that can guide us to deeper, more meaningful lives.

Ketuvim, meaning "Writings," is the name of the third section of the Hebrew Scriptures. Along with Torah (the first five books of the Bible: Genesis, Exodus, Leviticus, Numbers, and Deuteronomy) and NeviꞋim (meaning "Prophets," including the books of Joshua, Judges, Samuel, Kings, Isaiah, Jeremiah, Ezekiel, Hosea, Joel, Amos, Obadiah, Jonah, Micah, Nahum, Habakkuk, Zephaniah, Haggai, Zechariah, and Malachi), this third section comprises the Hebrew Scriptures (known in the Christian world as the Old Testament). Included in Ketuvim are Psalms, Proverbs, Job, Song of Songs, Ruth, Lamentations, Ecclesiastes, Esther, Daniel, Ezra-Nehemiah, and Chronicles. As Bible detectives, we need to unearth what is at the heart of each of these books. We need to look at why they are grouped together and, even more importantly, how we can raise the quality of our daily lives through their understanding.

Written primarily in ancient Hebrew, the original texts contain subtleties that are easily lost in translation. To explore the texts deeply, we will need to look at some of these double meanings that may be found in specific words. The translations used here are from the Jewish Publication Society's Tanakh, the ArtScroll Tanach by Mesorah Publishing, the Soncino Edition of the Babylonian Talmud, the Schottenstein Edition of the Babylonian Talmud, or my own direct translations of the Hebrew.[2] Similarly, these ancient writings use multiple Hebrew words for the name of God. In the Kabbalistic (Jewish mystical) tradition, each of these names has a different connotation, which we will not be exploring, as it is beyond the scope of this book. But it is important to recognize that God is beyond being either "feminine" or "masculine," and I have attempted to use language that reflects that understanding of Divinity. While using anthropomorphic terms is helpful for many people when referring to God, it can also be a setback, and so I have also used terms such as Divine, Life, or the Universe to reflect the infinite nature of God. Any reference to the Divine as "he" or "she" here is merely for the sake of ease and has no connotation of gender. As Rabbi J. B. Sacks is fond of saying, when he refers to God as "he," "I figure that God's a big girl and she can take care of herself."

Perhaps the first item we need to examine in our exploration is the compilation of the books themselves, and their order within Ketuvim. In today's Bible, they are ordered in the way listed above. Intellectually, this makes sense. Psalms, Proverbs, and Job are written in a similar style, with all being books of "poetry." Song of Songs, Ruth, Lamentations, Ecclesiastes, and Esther are called the Megillot—scrolls that are each read on different Jewish holidays. Song of Songs is read on the holiday of Passover; Ruth on Shavuot, the holiday commemorating the giving of Torah on Mount Sinai; Lamentations is read on Tisha B'Av, the holiday mourning the destruction of the temple in Jerusalem; Ecclesiastes is read during Sukkot, the holiday remembering the forty years the Hebrews spent wandering in the desert; and Esther is read on Purim, a holiday teaching of excess, persecution, and redemption. Daniel, Ezra-Nehemiah, and Chronicles are considered the "other books" of Ketuvim, as they don't fit into either of the previous two groups. This is an order that makes sense, has meaning, and is easily understood.

But this is not the order of the books as they were originally canonized. Let's take a look at what the original order was, and then, with some investigation, we may be able to evaluate each of the books and the entire group more clearly.

Of Talmuds, Targums, Texts, and Traditions

The earliest record of the Bible's canonization is found in the Talmud. Also known as the Oral Torah, this collection of writings was assembled between the second and fifth centuries of the Common Era. Originally taught orally, it is an ancient tradition that some of the text of this great work dates back all the way to Moses and Mount Sinai. *Pirkei Avot*, one of these tractates of Talmud whose name translates to "Teachings of Our Fathers," states, "Moses received the Torah at Sinai and transmitted it to Joshua, Joshua to the Elders, and the Elders to the Prophets, and the Prophets to the Men of the Great Assembly" (*Pirkei Avot* 1:1, Schottenstein). Fearing that these oral teachings would be lost, the head of the Great Assembly in the second century, Judah HaNasi (Judah the Prince), codified and assembled these teachings into the Mishnah, which became the foundation of the Talmud. The discussions found in the Talmud give us insight into the dialogues and debates about law, ethics, customs, and history as understood at that time.

The importance of the Talmud when unearthing the hidden meanings of the Bible cannot be overestimated. Many things in the Bible are not clearly explained in the text itself and can only be understood in conjunction with the Talmudic understanding. A simple way to understand this importance is with the following traditional example. God tells Moses to write down "Remember the sabbath day" (Exod 20:8, JPS). God then verbally explains to Moses what it means to "remember" the Sabbath. Moses passes that oral understanding to Joshua, who passes it to the elders, and so on. Hundreds of years later, like in any game of "telephone," there are discussions among the men of the Great Assembly about what was really said to Moses, and then further dialogues about the hidden meanings and how they relate to the human condition. Those dialogues are the foundation of a series of more intense and in-depth discussions and laws that become codified as the "Talmud."

Each section, or tractate, of the Talmud deals with different issues and themes. Tractate *Bava Batra* deals primarily with a person's rights and responsibilities of ownership. Yet, on page 14b of this tractate, we find an interesting discussion between the sages of the Talmud:

> The order of the Writings is Ruth, and the book of Psalms, and Job, and Proverbs, Ecclesiastes, the Song of Songs, and

Lamentations, Daniel, and the Scroll of Esther, Ezra, and Chronicles.

This is a very different order than what we are accustomed to today. By medieval times, the current order of today was used by the Jews of Germany, probably dating back to customs of the ninth century. While this more modern sequence is based on literary style and holiday celebrations, it is the original order as described in the Talmud that will allow us to understand these texts at deeper levels, and enable us to explore and investigate some of the potentially life-changing teachings in Ketuvim.

Before proceeding with our investigation, there is another crucial piece to understand, again coming from a line in the Talmud. It was the custom of the ancients to write a *Targum* of biblical text. A Targum is a translation and commentary on the text in the spoken language of the time; in the times of Talmud this was Aramaic. This was to help with the study and understanding of the text. Oldest are the targumim of Targum Onkelos, a translation and commentary on the Torah; and Targum Jonathan ben Uzziel, a commentary on the Prophets section of the Bible. We find this in the Talmudic tractate *Megillah* on page 3a:

> The *Targum* of the Pentateuch was composed by Onkelos the proselyte under the guidance of R. Eleazar and R. Joshua. The *Targum* of the Prophets was composed by Jonathan ben Uzziel under the guidance of Haggai, Zechariah and Malachi, and the land of Israel [thereupon] quaked over an area of four hundred *parasangs* by four hundred *parasangs*, and a *Bath Kol* (heavenly voice) came forth and exclaimed, Who is this that has revealed My secrets to mankind? Jonathan b. Uzziel thereupon arose and said, It is I who have revealed Thy secrets to mankind. It is fully known to Thee that I have not done this for my own honour or for the honour of my father's house, but for Thy honour I have done it, that dissension may not increase in Israel. He further sought to reveal [by] a *targum* [the inner meaning] of the Hagiographa [Ketuvim], but a *Bath Kol* went forth and said, Enough! What was the reason?—Because the date of the Messiah is foretold in it. (Soncino)

Although countless commentaries on Ketuvim were created subsequent to this Talmudic discussion, there has never been an "official" Targum as a result of this passage. This book is also not a Targum, and it would be arrogant to think that we can even begin to explore the inner meanings of the Ketuvim with the depth and understanding of Jonathan ben Uzziel. But, by exploring together the text through a different lens than it is traditionally understood, perhaps we can begin to glean some of the depth and wisdom that is truly hidden in these Writings.

We will probably never know what Jonathan ben Uzziel would have explained to future generations. But by careful analysis of the text, the original order of the books, and the unifying theme that ties through all of them, it may be possible to understand and utilize the Ketuvim in a practical way that increases our awareness of our relationship with God.

And it is that relationship lying at the heart of all these books. Ketuvim is not about understanding God as a "noun" or even as a "verb" but experiencing God directly through relationships. Each of the books teaches us how to experience God in a variety of circumstances, in a multiplicity of situations. Through Ketuvim, we can learn how to not only see but also experience the Divine in every aspect of Life—in every moment. We can learn to be "present," to transcend pain into peace, and to be conscious of God's hand in each and every instant.

How do these books teach us to experience God in every relationship? Why is this a valid lens with which to understand these texts? The answer is in the exploration. With investigation, we will find that each of these books deals with a uniquely different opportunity of experiencing God in relationship. Ruth teaches us to experience God in the relationship between mentor and mentee, between elder and youth, between parent and child. Psalms guides us to know God as we experience the emotions and feelings that are such an integral part of the human experience. Job shows us how to know God in the midst of suffering, and Proverbs helps us learn to experience God in the midst of a community. Ecclesiastes goes even a step further, guiding us to experience God in all aspects of Life. Song of Songs is the ultimate handbook about knowing God through an intimate relationship with an other, and Lamentations reminds us of how to face God in the midst of pain. Daniel, considered a difficult book for scholars and clergy for thousands of years, teaches us to know and experience God in the relationship that we have with time itself; while the scroll of Esther reminds us of how to know God even when he/she seems not to be there and/or when there are issues of addiction and excessive behavior patterns. Ezra-Nehemiah and Chronicles take all this information about experiencing God in relationships and anchor it back into physical actions. Each of these texts is a guide into directly experiencing God in every possible relationship, in every possible way, and adjusting our behavior and actions as a result.

The understandings and interpretations of the texts as presented here are gleaned from a variety of sources and traditions, both ancient and modern. Sometimes, the understandings may reflect one specific faith tradition or denomination's view. Occasionally, they are not entirely consonant with the "normative" Jewish commentaries or viewing perspective usually presented by rabbis, ministers, and academics. Nowhere in this book is this truer than in the chapter on Esther. The interpretation presented here, while valid, important, and extremely useful in the twenty-first century, is by no means the majority opinion historically. The interpretation of the book of Esther is usually presented as a story of courage and redemption, a story of the heroism of both Esther and Mordecai. This is not only the more common understanding but is also accurate: they are heroes, and God saved the Jewish people from a persecution. Yet, part of the premise of the book in your hands is that these texts have many meanings simultaneously, and it is an entirely different meaning that is gleaned from the book of Esther here than you would find in a typical commentary. This is not meant to denigrate or infer that the more normative interpretation is inaccurate, but rather to deepen and add to the more common understandings. With Esther, and with any of the other books examined here, it is up to readers to find the more "classic" commentaries if they choose, and I recommend it wholeheartedly. *Bamidbar Rabbah* 13:15 teaches that there are seventy different interpretations (literally, "seventy faces") of any text, and the contents of this book are meant to enhance and deepen the reader's personal experience of Ketuvim, so that these ancient words can enhance your daily life.

Two thousand years ago, Jonathan ben Uzziel explained and helped all people understand the section of Prophets through his monumental work. As he said, it was so "that dissension may not increase in Israel." Perhaps by investigating the Ketuvim more thoroughly and by delving deeply into these books of wisdom, we too can prevent dissension from increasing in our own lives and, as a result, in the world.

Now, let us start to explore. . . .

Note

1. This book uses a couple of special characters in the transliteration of Hebrew words, none of which present difficulties for pronunciation but they are good to know nonetheless. The ʾ (as in *Neviʾim*) denotes the aleph (א). This letter is silent, acting as a placeholder for whatever vowel that follows it. An apostrophe (ʾ) denotes a contraction of a preposition or conjunction with a noun. For instance, *B'shalom* means "with peace" and *B'shalom u'vracha* means "with peace and blessings."

2. In citations, these are indicated as JPS, ArtScroll, Soncino, and Schottenstein, respectively.

1

Ruth: The First Interpersonal Relationship

Whither thou goest, I will go; and where thou lodgest, I will lodge; thy people shall be my people, and thy God my God.

—Ruth 1:16 (American Standard Version)

Ruth and Naomi

The story of Ruth and Naomi is one of the most beautiful relationships in the Hebrew Scriptures. The story is simple and elegant, with a multitude of hidden meanings if we are willing to really turn the text over.

The story of the book takes place in the "days when the Judges judged" (Ruth 1:1, ArtScroll). It is before the time of the kings in Israel, and there is a famine occurring in the land of Israel. Elimelech, a great man from Judah, travels with his wife Naomi from Bethlehem to Moab with their two sons, Mahlon and Chilion. Elimelech dies, and Naomi's sons marry two Moabite women: Orpah and Ruth. Some years later, Mahlon and Chilion also die, and Naomi chooses to return to Judah when she hears that the famine is over.

Naomi encourages both her daughters-in-law to leave her, to return to their people, and to be blessed with rich lives. Both young women wish to stay with Naomi, but Orpah relents after Naomi tells her again to leave. Ruth, however, chooses to stay with her mother-in-law, creating one of the deepest of relationships in the Bible. The two women return to Bethlehem, and Ruth goes to collect the gleanings of the fields that are left for widows and orphans. There, Ruth meets the owner of the fields, Boaz, who is much older than she. Boaz is also related to Elimelech and, as such, has an obligation to both redeem and take care of Naomi and Ruth. Boaz is helpful to Ruth and invites her to keep gleaning in his fields so that she can be under his protection.

Naomi realizes that she must help Ruth gain security in life, and so Naomi guides her daughter-in-law to approach Boaz, and ultimately to convince him to redeem them. Using Naomi's advice, Ruth becomes intimate with Boaz, who publicly redeems and marries her. They have a child, Obed, who becomes the grandfather of King David; the neighborhood women say, "A son is born to Naomi," as Ruth lets her mother-in-law raise the child (4:17, JPS).

The book of Ruth is a simple and elegant story of a woman who has seemingly lost everything, only to find life again in the relationship with her daughter-in-law. Although the main character is Naomi, the book itself is about Ruth's journey from Moabite to widow to wife to mother. Throughout it all, there is a clear and strong relationship between Naomi and Ruth, and it is in the understanding of this relationship that we will be able to glean other meanings from the text.

The Primary Human Relationship of Parenthood

The first relationship that almost every child experiences is that with a parent, specifically a mother. It is through this relationship that the child first comes to understand God in whatever terms. "God" is too big to understand, but the mother who supplies physical and emotional nourishment is the first cognitive understanding of Divinity. Many studies by psychologists place such importance on this primary relationship that they believe that a person's entire ethical behavioral system is developed by the age of three: all based on the first interactions with the elder.

This is the first relationship we find explored in Ketuvim: the relationship of a daughter and a mother. Although technically Ruth is a daughter-in-law, Naomi calls Ruth a "daughter." Naomi, while not her physical mother, is Ruth's "spiritual" mother. Through this relationship and love, Ruth chooses to be reborn as a Hebrew, a convert to Judaism, because of her love for Naomi. Naomi opens up her eyes to experiencing God in the ways of the Israelites (rather than the Moabite idol worship that Ruth grew up with). This mother-daughter relationship becomes the first model of experiencing God directly—so directly that Ruth commits her entire well-being and life to be with Naomi, to explore that relationship, and to knowing God through that relationship. "Thy people shall be my people, and thy God my God," says Ruth to her mother-in-law.

As children get a bit older, they are able to relate to other elders, uncles and aunts, teachers, and mentors. Ruth mirrors this in her own spiritual development. As they journey together, Naomi becomes more of a mentor as opposed to only a mother for Ruth, and guides the young woman in multiple ways. She instructs Ruth to glean from the fields, to stay close to Boaz, and to ultimately go to Boaz in the middle of the night. Through her guidance, Ruth grows into a strong woman who develops her own relationship with Boaz, eventually becoming his wife. From this union comes the grandfather of David, the king of Israel, who not only unifies the kingdom but from whose loins the Messiah is foretold to be descended.

How can we take this understanding of the relationship between Ruth and Naomi and utilize it in our own lives? The easiest way is perhaps to compare Ruth with Naomi's other daughter-in-law, Orpah. Orpah also expresses a desire to stay with Naomi, but quickly succumbs and goes back to her homeland. Ruth, on the other hand, realizes the depth of her relationship and understands on some level the spiritual awakening into which Naomi has already guided her. She not only commits her physical body to stay with her mentor but places her spiritual well-being in the hands of Naomi as well.

Naomi, the Life Coach

For some people of the twenty-first century, this may seem like a form of surrendering one's own personality and free will, but this is not the case. This model of surrendering to the guidance of the mentor who opens up a spiritual awakening is found around the world in different religious and spiritual faith traditions. It is accepted in the yogic traditions that the "guru" knows more about the spiritual journey needed for the disciple than the disciple does, and the disciple must choose to exercise free will and surrender to the guru's guidance. Similarly, in the world of the Hasidic Jew, the "rebbe" is understood to know the needs of the Hasid better than the Hasid does, and so the Hasidic Jew lets go of his ego and attaches himself completely on a spiritual level with the rebbe. To become the shaman in many of the indigenous tribes of North, South, and Central America, the would-be disciple must demonstrate his ability to give up choosing anything other than accepting what the shaman tells him to do, all in order that his own awareness of Life increases so that he can someday become the shaman of the tribe. The pattern is consistent throughout the world and exemplified by the relationship of Ruth and Naomi. Ruth gives up her own previous identity to attach herself to Naomi, and in doing this she will ultimately come to her destiny to not only marry Boaz but also to be the mother of the ancestor of both the great King David and the future Messiah.

As adults in modern times, it is often difficult to surrender our free will, and it is *never* appropriate to have it taken from us. Notice that Naomi tries to convince her daughters to leave her; she does not try to encourage them to follow her. She even uses every argument that she can to convince Ruth not to follow her:

> Turn back, my daughters; why will you go with me? Are there yet any more sons in my womb, that they may be your husbands? Turn back, my daughters, go your way; for I am too old to have a husband. If I should say, I have hope, even if I should have a husband tonight, and should bear sons. Would you wait for them till they were grown? Would you, for them, refrain from having husbands? No, my daughters; for it grieves me much for your sakes that the hand of the Lord is gone out against me. (Ruth 1:11-14, ArtScroll)

It is not a "cult of the personality" wherein Naomi makes all sorts of promises of fame, fortune, and fun to Orpah and Ruth; rather she clearly tries to dissuade them from staying with her. In Orpah's case, she is successful. But even though it is difficult for Ruth, she chooses to follow and attach herself to Naomi, despite the discouragement. This is one of the keys to understanding the appropriate mentor-mentee relationship: be wary if the "guide" wants a "disciple" too much. We learn through this text that the real Guide doesn't want disciples but will accept them when they commit fully to the journey together.

The text teaches us that once we have attached ourselves to a guide/guru/rebbe/mentor, we must then trust that person completely. Although on the surface it may appear that Ruth gave up her own free will, in reality she made the deepest of decisions by choosing to surrender to Naomi's guidance. Even when Naomi tells Ruth to go to Boaz and lie by his feet, her daughter-in-law does this without hesitation (Ruth 3:4). Despite the challenging implications of Naomi's instruction, Ruth's only reply is "All that you say to me I will do" (Ruth 3:5, ArtScroll). From this eventually comes the union and commitment of Boaz to Ruth. If Ruth had argued with Naomi, or chosen to do anything other than what Naomi told her, she would not have ended up being married to Boaz, nor would she have been the ancestor of the Messiah.

It is this aspect of Ruth's commitment to the relationship with Naomi that needs to be explored to see how it teaches us to experience God. Once we have attached ourselves to a guide, it is imperative that we trust him or her fully, even more than our own mothers. In some circles of Judaism, there is greater respect paid to one's teachers than even to one's parents. While the parents are responsible for the physical growth of the child, the teachers are responsible for the spiritual and intellectual growth. As such, they are given extra honors. When we accept a teacher upon ourselves, we must choose to surrender to his or her wisdom as a guide. It is only in doing this, as we see from Ruth's commitment to doing what Naomi instructed, that we can come to our ultimate "destiny."

What wisdom do we learn from this text of Ruth? We learn to attach ourselves to a spiritual teacher, a mentor—a "mother" (or "father"). We can identify mentors by their commitment to their own tradition (Naomi, although poor and a widow, decides to return to Israel), their commitment to discouraging us from following them, and their willingness to take responsibility for the relationship if we persist. We learn through this text that surrendering free will in favor of accepting guidance from a mentor can be extremely difficult on many levels, but also fruitful and valuable. By attaching ourselves to one who is wiser, and who has introduced and guided us into a deeper spiritual awakening, we can experience God in the fulfillment of our destiny. Through this primary relationship of child to parent, and then student to a teacher or guide, we can directly experience God in our lives: in our workplace (Ruth's gleanings of the field support her and Naomi), in our families (Ruth ultimately becomes married to Boaz), and in our soul's purpose. Ruth goes from being a young widow to becoming the great-grandmother of a king and the ancestor of the Messiah, all through her relationship with Naomi. The text asks us to surrender, to learn, to grow, and to see the results of God's interactions with us through our own relationship with elders.

The Talmud teaches, "Make for yourself a teacher, acquire for yourself a friend, and judge all men in the scale of merit" (*Pirkei Avot* 1:6, Schottenstein). There is no more primary relationship that we can have, no relationship that can open the door to experiencing God directly in our daily lives, that is simpler and deeper than the interpersonal relationship of teacher-student, parent-child, and mentor-mentee. Attach yourself to that teacher as Ruth did, acquire friends as a result of your learning from that mentor, and then you will truly experience God so fully that you will be able to judge all humans based on the scale of their true merit, and what was "fate" will become the hand of God moving you into your own destiny.

2

Psalms:
Experiencing God within Every Feeling

Let every soul praise Yah,
Praise God!
　　　　　　　—Psalm 150

I've heard there was a secret chord
That David played, and it pleased the Lord.
　　　　　　　—Leonard Cohen, "Hallelujah"*

The book of Psalms is arguably the most used and shared text by spiritual traditions around the world. Traditionally attributed to King David and called *Tehillim* ("praises" in Hebrew), this book is composed of 150 distinct songs or poems (a few are attributed in the text *Shir HaShirim Rabbah* to ten earlier leaders such as Moses, and modern academics place their origin at a slightly later time period and by multiple authors). Originally meant to be played on the harp and sung, verses from the psalms appear in

* *Various Positions*, Sony Music Entertainment (Canada), 1984.

nearly every Jewish and Christian service. Excerpts from Psalm 145 (known as *Ashrei*) are said every day, and it is the custom among many Jews to recite Psalms 145–150 each day as part of their daily practice. When a person has died, a *shomer* (guardian) stays at the side of the deceased until burial, reciting psalms; and the Twenty-Third Psalm is recited at nearly every funeral in both Judaism and Christianity.

These writings are considered powerful in multiple other traditions and rituals as well, and are an important part of nearly every Christian denomination's practices. The Catholic Church's Liturgy of the Hours has at its centerpiece the recitation of psalms. The Anglican Church's Psalter is at the heart of that church's liturgy; the hymns (psalms put to musical arrangements) are an important part of every Protestant denomination from Presbyterian to Rastafarian. Even in the Muslim world, these words are taken as sacred text, with the traditional Islamic point of view being that God dictated these to David directly in the same way that the Torah was given to Moses, and the Qurʾan to Mohammed.

One of the most beautiful understandings of the psalms is found in the teachings of Rebbe Nachman of Breslov (1772–1810), the great Hasidic mystic. Rebbe Nachman teaches of the *Tikkun HaKlali*, the "General Remedy," which is a recitation of ten individual psalms (Pss 16, 32, 41, 42, 59, 77, 90, 105, 137, and 150). According to this great rabbi, all physical ailments have at their root a spiritual imbalance, and this General Remedy can heal all flaws and sicknesses:

> There are places that are so fine and narrow that no remedy has the power to penetrate them except through the General Remedy, which injects healing into even the narrowest, finest places. First it is necessary to apply the General Remedy, and through this all the individual flaws will automatically be rectified. It is true that the General Remedy is higher and more exalted than all the individual remedies. (Nachman, *Likutey Mohoran*)[1]

These words are a part of so many traditions, and clearly are considered to be powerful, but what are they really about? What ties them together, and how can they be used to deepen our relationship with God?

The Psalms as Literature

Structurally and stylistically, the psalms can be placed into a few different groups. There are psalms of praise (also often referred to by Christians as "hymns"), psalms of lament, psalms of petition, psalms of thanksgiving, and psalms that refer directly to an event or time in King David's life. Like many of the popular songs of today, parallelism is often used to convey ideas in song or poetic form. A concept is made clearer either by repeating it in different words or by juxtaposing a second sentence that is antithetical to the first:

> God will protect you from every evil,
> He will guard your soul.
> He will guard your going and your coming,
> From now and forever. (Ps 121:7-8, ArtScroll)

> Though I walk through the valley of the shadow of death,
> I shall fear no evil, for you are with me. (Ps 23:4, ArtScroll)

But although this is the common structure and styles for the psalms, there is a much clearer theme that can be found in their content throughout. Each psalm is an expression of an emotion. Often the emotion is gratitude (psalms of thanksgiving), pain (psalms of lament), or joy (psalms of praise), but all the psalms are rich texts that describe the expression of a very human emotion in beautiful song form.

Perhaps this is why these words have transcended faith traditions and been such a source of inspiration for thousands of years. Like any of the popular songs of today, they are the expression of human feelings, but they have the unique ability to incorporate God into the emotional equation.

The Author of the Psalms:
King David, the Man of Passion

King David, as we learn about him in the Hebrew Scriptures and oral commentaries of Talmud, was a very "human" being. He was not "holier than thou," but rather a man of passion, anger, fear, and the entire gamut of human emotions. He was the youngest of eight sons, and considered by his family to be the least likely to succeed. When Samuel the prophet came to the house of Jesse and first saw Eliab, the eldest of Jesse, Samuel thought he had found the future king. But God disqualified not only Eliab but all the other brothers that were present as well (*Midrash Shmuel* 19). Finally, David was called in from the fields, where he was tending sheep. Samuel at first thought that David had the look of Esau—that is, the look of a killer—but the text of *Bereshit Rabbah* (66:3) tells us of God's understanding a different quality that was an inherent part of the young David:

> When Samuel first laid his eyes on David he was alarmed. He said, "This ruddy fellow is a bloody killer like Esau!" But the Holy One, Blessed be He, allayed Samuel's fears and said, "No! This one is different because he is with beautiful eyes. Esau murders to satisfy his own desires, but David slays his foes upon the advice and guidance of Sanhedrin, who are the eyes of the congregation."

David was "ruddy" (*admoni*), which is an outward expression of "burning passions tamed only with effort" (*Ohr Hachaim HaKodosh*; Deut 31:1). His very nature was one of feeling, and then acting on those feelings. We see David repeat this pattern throughout his life, from his time as the passionate singer of Israel to King Saul, to his time as a guerrilla warrior, through his relationships with both Jonathan and Bathsheba, all the way to his old age and death. The one word that may most describe David is "passion," and he brought that fire to everything that he did. He felt everything deeply, whether it was anger or fear, joy or ecstasy, desire or regret.

The king conveyed those feelings in the amazing lyrics and music that became the psalms. Like the great songwriters and performers of today, King David put words to the deepest of feelings that are found in the human condition. And like the great musicians of today, he at times let his personal passions become a form of self-sabotage. But uniquely in history, David was able to find God in all his highly charged emotional experiences and to convey that Divinity in his songs: the psalms.

Psalms are not just songs of praise, thanksgiving, or lament. They are the expressions of a man in the midst of deep feelings who finds God within those emotions. They are the words of a man in the midst of emotional turmoil and excess but who experiences God within those feelings. They are the songs of a man feeling deeply alone or deeply joyous, but always with God as a part of the equation of the feelings.

From the time that we are children, we are taught how to manage our emotions so that they can be expressed "appropriately." But for most people, there are times when those emotions are so powerful, so deep, that there is no appropriate way to express them. King David teaches us a different model, the model of experiencing God within each of the deep emotions of the human experience.

Using the Psalms to See Divinity in Emotions

Let's take an example of the genius of King David, and how his words are part of the expression of one of the deepest human emotions: grief. As a rabbi who is blessed with the task of helping many families through the grieving and mourning process, I have personally experienced the challenge so many people face in expressing themselves at a funeral. The emotions are so deep, the loss so great, that it is easy to get lost in eulogizing a loved one. I often suggest to people to think twice before speaking at a loved one's funeral, as it is so easy to get lost in the feelings that it can become oppressive to the other people attending the funeral.

We've all attended those funerals where a loved one gets up to "say a few words" and a half hour later is still talking, trying so hard to express in words what can never be fully said about the loss they are feeling for their loved one. But King David gives us words that somehow bring comfort and strength and are so powerful that they are used at almost every funeral—the Twenty-Third Psalm:

> The Lord is my shepherd
> I shall not want
> He makes me to lie down in green pastures
> He leads me beside the still waters
> He restores my soul
> He guides me in right paths for His name's sake
> Though I walk in the valley of the shadow of death
> I will fear no evil, for You are with me
> Your rod and your staff, they comfort me
> You spread a table before me in the presence of my enemies
> You anoint my head with oil
> My cup runneth over
> Only goodness and mercy shall follow me
> All the days of my life
> And I shall dwell in the house of the Lord forever.
>   (ArtScroll)

This psalm, possibly the most familiar piece in the book, is recited over and over when people need comfort. Ironically, many people believe at first that it is a psalm to honor the deceased, but, in fact, it is a beautiful piece that reminds us in our pain that God is always present. Even when we are in deep fear (it is a common reaction to experience fear of death when at the funeral of a loved one), these words comfort us. They remind us that God is not absent but is present even in these painful moments. Psalm 23 is King David's reminder to us that we should remember that even in the midst of our pain and fear, goodness and mercy follow us all the days of our lives, and we shall dwell in God's house forever. When we realize and accept that God is comforting us mercifully even in the midst of death, then the fear that we had becomes a deep sense of awe in the beauty of the Divine. (In Hebrew, the same word means both "fear" and "awe.") Through David's beautiful words, we can access our own awareness of Divinity in the relationship that we have with pain and fear. King David helps us to find God in the midst of grief.

Sometimes our grief and pain is so overwhelming that it becomes almost desperate. Most people have experienced this in one way or another. A consecutive series of losses, possibly of a job, relationship, and then a loved one's death, can create emotional pain within a person that is so large that he or she literally cannot function. Or it could be just one huge loss that creates a vacuum, a void, inside of our souls. The phrase "dark night of the soul" (taken from the poem of the same name by the Carmelite priest St. John of the Cross) is truly the appropriate term. As Buddhist teacher and author Jack Engler has said, "There is instinctive coiling and withdrawal; nothing seems sufficiently worth doing or caring about."[2] Often we feel paralyzed, incapable of feeling anything except the pain of desperation and loneliness, almost as if we have been abandoned by everyone, everything, and even God.

But there are psalms that help us to see Divinity in these times when it seems that everyone has conspired against us. When we feel desperate and abused by all of Life. Words that help us get through this painful part of our life journey:

> For see, they lie in wait for me;
> fierce men plot against me
> for no offense of mine,
> for no transgression, O Lord;
> for no guilt of mine
> do they rush to array themselves against me.

> Look, rouse Yourself on my behalf!
> You, O Lord God of hosts,
> God of Israel,
> bestir Yourself to bring all nations to account;
> have no mercy on any treacherous villain. . . .

They come each evening growling like dogs,
roaming the city.
They wander in search of food;
and whine if they are not satisfied.
But I will sing of Your strength,
extol each morning Your faithfulness;
For You have been my haven,
a refuge in time of trouble.

O my strength, to You I sing hymns
for God is my haven, my faithful God.
        (Ps 59:2-6, 15-18, ArtScroll)

The psalmist here freely and fully expresses his feeling that the world has turned against him, and gives us the key to experiencing God in the midst of this darkness. He gives voice to his pain and then plaintively reminds himself that God has always been there before and is still there. As is echoed in the famous poem "Footprints in the Sand,"[3] the psalm reminds us that it is specifically when we feel alone that, in fact, God is most supporting us:

"Why, when I needed you most, you have not been there for
    me?"
The Lord replied,
"The times when you have seen only one set of footprints in
    the sand
is when I carried you."

In the same way that Psalm 23 reminded us of God's presence in our moments of grief, Psalm 59 and those like it remind us that God is an active part of our relationship when we feel that we are being persecuted in whatever way and are truly suffering. This psalm again gives us a model: express the pain, frustration, and fear, and then recognize the great gifts that you have been given prior to this dark night. In remembering and honoring those gifts, we start to get a sense of gratitude that will allow us to journey through the dark night into the deep joy of Life that comes afterward.

Gratitude, Praise, and Happiness

A sense of gratitude not only can take us through the dark night, as illustrated above, but it is also one of the keys to happiness. There is an "exercise" that I first heard of from Rabbi Noah Weinberg, the founder of Aish HaTorah, called a "gratitude journal." In assigning it to hundreds of students over the years as part of a class, I consistently heard back that it was one of the most powerful teachings of the semester. The idea is to take a journal and spend a full hour writing everything that you are grateful for in your life. (Generally, the first fifteen minutes are easy, the second fifteen minutes are tough, the third fifteen minutes are extremely difficult, and during the fourth fifteen minutes it can be difficult to not be cursing at the person who told you about the process.) Then, each morning, add a new thing to your gratitude list, and again in the evening before you go to sleep. After a period of time, gratitude has become such a large part of your life that it affects every experience that you encounter.

I had been doing this exercise for a few years when my mother informed me that she had been diagnosed with ovarian cancer. That evening, I added to the journal that I was grateful for experiencing the pain of being close to a cancer patient. It was incredibly painful and scary, but through this exercise I had realized that many things that may seem like curses are actually experiences that help us grow tremendously. When she died a few months later, just two weeks before my rabbinic ordination, I wrote in the journal that I was grateful for the new feeling of being without a parent. Again, it was scary and excruciatingly painful, but by being grateful, I was aware of the pain without suffering in it. Gratitude takes away suffering, and can also create happiness.

Expressions of gratitude are powerful parts of many psalms and help us to embody more gratitude and, as a result, more happiness in our lives. Often it is as simple as recognizing and being grateful for the miracles of nature:

> The world stands firm;
> It cannot be shaken.

Your throne stands firm from of old;
From eternity You have existed.
The ocean sounds, O Lord,
The ocean sounds its thunder,
The ocean sounds its pounding.
Above the thunder of the mighty waters,
More majestic than the breakers of the sea
Is the Lord, majestic on high. (Ps 93:1-4, ArtScroll)

Taking the first step of being grateful for the most basic aspects of nature ultimately creates a sense of joy within every aspect of a person's life. And that happiness has a magnificent depth, being founded on the realization that God is present in everything, making the ordinary become extraordinary. More consistently than any writings in history, the psalms help us to remember the presence of God in all of Life. As a result, we start to feel true joy in each moment.

Grief, fear, anger, desperation, gratitude: these are some of the primary emotions that every person feels at some point. Through the use of the psalms, we can transcend these powerful feelings and transform them into joy as we recognize and experience God in each moment. This may be the greatest gift from these magnificent poems: that by realizing God is present in all of our feelings, we can experience true happiness on a consistent basis. When we have this joy and gratitude in our lives, there is little we can do but praise, and perhaps that is why Psalm 150, the last song of the book, is so full of joyous praise:

Hallelujah
Praise God in His sanctuary
Praise Him in the sky, His stronghold
Praise Him for His mighty acts
Praise Him for His exceeding greatness
Praise Him with blasts of the horn
Praise Him with harp and lyre
Praise Him with timbrel and dance
Praise Him with lute and pipe
Praise Him with resounding cymbals
Praise Him with loud-clashing cymbals

Let every soul that breathes praise God
Hallelujah
(ArtScroll)

This is the great genius of David's songs. When we become aware that God is part of the relationship we have with every feeling, from pain to fear, from desperation to joy, we feel that deep sense of gratitude, and our only response is to be joyous in our praise of God and all of Life.

What If?

Play a game for a moment. Let go of your mind, and everything that you "know" to be true. Imagine, just imagine, for this moment that everything is being choreographed for you. Especially for you. The sounds around you are exactly what your soul needs at this moment. The wind, the colors, the people passing by, and the snippets of conversation that you hear are being choreographed right now by the Creator of all specifically for your benefit. Magnificently, you are also part of the gifts to everyone else around you in this moment. The most perfect and powerful expression of love is becoming manifested for you in this very moment, and in every moment. Really imagine this, and feel how amazing it is to be loved so deeply. Is there really any other response to that overwhelming feeling of truly being treasured other than to be profoundly grateful, and to praise that love?

King David did not just imagine that feeling; he experienced it. In his life he traversed from the depths of pain to the highest ecstasies. Because God was always a part of the equation, he was able to write the stirring words that are still so important in so many religions.

So how do you use these songs, these poems, found in the book of Psalms, in your life? First, you become familiar with at least a few of them, to prepare yourself for when they are needed. Then, when you are feeling something so overwhelming that you have no sense of God in your life for whatever reason, begin to read the psalms. Read the ones you have become familiar with, and follow David's journey from a shepherd to a warrior to a great king, from feelings of darkness into an awareness of light. Travel with King David through his words. Don't just read the psalms, but let them move through you a word at a time. Relate to the feelings as deeply as you can, and let the words then guide you into the awareness that God is everywhere and in every feeling. Gratitude will then start to take hold of you, and guide you into a feeling of joy.

By doing this you will find, a step at a time, that your personal human experience will have more of a sense of including the Divine. And you will know that God is with you. Always. In all of your emotions. Hallelujah.

Notes

1. Avraham Greenbaum, trans., *The Wings of the Sun* (Brooklyn: Moznaim Publishing, 1985).

2. "Practice for Awakening" (lecture, Barre Center for Buddhist Studies, November 1, 1997).

3. Although this poem is most often credited to Mary Stevenson, there is a debate about the actual authorship, with at least four other people also claiming authorship.

3

Job: Transforming Suffering into Love

Pain is inevitable. Suffering is optional.
> —Buddhist teaching from the Noble Eightfold Path*

Rabbis and academics alike constantly refer to the book of Job as the most commented on book in the entire Bible. Whether this is accurate or not, it is difficult to find a major biblical commentator who has not deeply explored this painful and challenging book. It is challenging, not just to the emotions but to the very heart of a person's faith and belief, through its exploration of the question, Why do good people suffer?

What Did I Do to Deserve This?

The story is relatively simple: Job was a righteous man living in the land of Utz in an unspecified time. He was of "unquestioning integrity coupled with a probing mind, he stood in awe of

---

* A Buddhist teaching and practice taught by Siddhartha Gautama designed to end suffering.

God and eschewed evil" (Job 1:1, ArtScroll). Successful in all ways, he had been blessed with three daughters and seven sons, as well as large amounts of possessions. Having introduced Job, the book moves into a dialogue between God and Satan (in this text, Satan is not considered "the Devil," but rather the "prosecuting Angel"). God brags to Satan about how pious and faithful Job is, and Satan then points out that this may only be true because he is so blessed by God. In fact, points out Satan, if you take away everything from him, he will curse God to his face. God gives Satan permission to hurt Job in any way that does not harm him personally, and Job loses his possessions and his children. But he still does not curse God. Satan then makes the argument that this is because Job is not in pain himself, and God agrees that Satan can do anything that he wants as long as he spares Job's life. Job is then covered with painful sores and expresses his lack of understanding for his suffering. He is visited by friends, each of whom tries to justify what is happening to Job. But none of their arguments resonate with Job, who knows that he has done nothing wrong and is not deserving of this pain. Ultimately, God comes and speaks with Job, points out some of the inadequacies of Job's understanding in comparison to the wisdom of the Infinite, chastises Job's friends for their lack of understanding and compassion, and then rewards Job with even more riches and children than he had before this journey began.

From the book of Job we not only get all sorts of theological and philosophical interpretations about the imminent presence of God (or lack thereof), but we are also forced to deal with the seeming contradiction of a God of "good" that allows and even encourages suffering. On a practical level, we also find the root of many of the practices around mourning, and how to comfort a mourner or a sick person. It is from this book that we find the classic line, "God gave, God took, blessed is the Name of God" (Job 1:21, ArtScroll), that is recited at almost every funeral, and learn about a mourner tearing his clothes. It is here we learn that we should not initiate conversation with a mourner but should wait for him or her to start the conversation, a practice still observed by many religious people today. The practices learned are useful, but much less so than the wrestling with the deep question of personal faith when confronted with suffering.

For any person of faith, this book is problematic. Job is not a bad person and has done nothing that is deserving of his suffering. He is honest in his defense of himself as a righteous man, and even Satan never says anything disparaging about Job's behavior. Job is a truly righteous and blameless man. So righteous, in fact, that in the book of Ezekiel, he is counted as one of the three greatest righteous men of all time, along with Noah and Daniel: "even if these three men—Noah, Daniel, and Job—should be in it [the land that has sinned against God], they would by their righteousness save only themselves—declares the Lord GOD" (Ezek 14:14, JPS).

Job's righteousness is a problem, given the tremendous suffering that he experiences. If we accept that he is truly righteous, then God seems capricious and almost sadistic in his treatment of Job. That definition of God is repulsive to many people, and certainly to the rabbis of long ago, and this may be why one Talmudic sage came up with a supposed "reason" to explain that Job was not quite as righteous as he seemed:

> Rabbi Hiyya bar Abba taught in Rabbi Simai's name: Three men were involved with Pharaoh's plan (to destroy Israel): Balaam, Job, and Jethro. Balaam, who advised Pharaoh to destroy the Jews was killed; Job, who kept silent, was stricken by suffering; Jethro, who fled was rewarded by having his descendants seated in the Chamber of Hewn Stone [as judges in the Sanhedrin]. (*Sotah* 11a, Schottenstein)

Here in the Oral Torah, the sages try to justify that Job really had done something bad: he had kept silent as an advisor of Pharaoh. When Pharaoh was considering what to do with the Hebrews immediately prior to the exodus from Egypt, Job kept silent. For his silence, he was punished with the suffering. The challenge with this explanation is that there is no indication within the book of Job itself that leads one to believe this, and the text says the exact opposite: that Job was blameless and righteous. Interestingly, this is one of the few places where the text of the Talmud does not just explain but directly contradicts what the written biblical text specifically says. Is this Talmudic explanation accurate, or is it merely an attempt to rationalize God's behavior without dealing with the underlying issues of God allowing the suffering to happen? This teaching from the Talmud clearly shows, at least, that as long as almost two thousand years ago, the great theologians of the time were trying to wrestle with the problem of Job's suffering and integrate it with their belief of an omnipotent, omnipresent, omniscient, and benevolent deity. This inherent issue within the book of Job causes significant debate within the early commentaries of the Talmud, even extending to the authorship of the text.

Page 15b of the Talmudic tractate *Bava Batra* contains numerous opinions regarding the true author of this challenging book, as well as the time in which he lived, as do other classic commentaries. Some of these opinions about him include the following points:

The text was written by Moses.

Job was a contemporary of Abraham.

He lived during the 210-year exile of the Hebrews in Egypt (*Midrash Rabbah Bereshit* 57).

He lived during the times of the spies of Israel who went into Canaan at the beginning of the 40 years of wandering.

He lived during the time of Jacob and married Jacob's daughter, Dinah.

He lived during the exile in Babylon, and established a house of study in Tiberias.

He lived in the days of Achashveirosh, the king in the book of Esther.

He lived during the reign of the Queen of Sheba, during the kingship of Solomon.

He lived during the time of King Nebuchadnezzar (Rashi's commentary).

He never really existed at all, and the entire story is to be taken as a parable to teach lessons.

We could obviously spend a tremendous amount of time trying to pinpoint the authorship and time frame of the historical Job. But if we're honest with ourselves, that easily becomes a distraction from dealing with the real issues and problems inherent in the text itself: Why and how can a good God allow a righteous person to suffer?

How Can God Let the Good Suffer?

The great modern commentator Rabbi Shimon Schwab poses this real issue of Job in elegant and simple terms:

> The central theme of Sefer Iyov [the book of Job] is the age-old problem of why the righteous suffer and the wicked succeed and prosper. Iyov focuses on the apparent disinterest of God when innocent people, and especially the righteous, suffer; and the fact that He allows the wicked to prosper.
>
> If a pattern existed in which all righteous people suffer, and all wicked people succeed and prosper, this would be indicative of a systematic method of reward and punishment. It could then be said that God causes the righteous to suffer in this world to expiate whatever sins they may have committed, so that they may receive their full reward in the World to Come, without having to suffer for their sins there. Similarly, if all wicked people were to prosper in this world, it could be understood as giving them their full reward for whatever good they may have done, leaving their punishment in its full fury—with no mitigation for their good deeds for the World to Come.
>
> However, no such pattern exists.[1]

Forgetting about authorship or even if there was a historical Job, the real subject is simple: Why do good people suffer? For a human being living in a world filled with suffering, this may be the largest obstacle to an individual having faith; and it is certainly one of the classic arguments of the atheist who uses it to demonstrate that God either does not exist or is capricious, cruel, and uninterested in humanity. Ultimately, the book of Job is less a story about God than it is about man and the human struggles with and in life.

How to Be Human in a Divine World

The book itself gives us a hint at the very beginning that this is an accurate assumption: that it is in actuality a book about mankind. Job is the only book of the Bible that begins with the word *ish*, meaning "man." If we examine the book closely, we can see from the outset that this is a piece of writing designed for humans, and applies not just to Jews, Christians, or people of faith, but to all mankind. But this makes sense given that the issue of suffering is one of the most primary and difficult subjects for a person to really explore. And it is just that topic that needs to be explored to achieve not only a deeper understanding of the text but also a deeper connection with God.

Job doesn't understand why all of this is happening to him, and desperately wants to plead his case before the Almighty, whom Job believes would change everything if he could understand how righteous Job really is. Job is joined by a few friends who try to comfort him in their own ways. In a series of speeches back and forth, these three friends, Eliphaz, Bildad, and Zophar, all try to convince Job that God has a straightforward formula: punish the wicked and reward the righteous. Their perspective is black and white: Job is suffering, therefore Job must have unknowingly sinned and must repent. Despite Job's protestations to each of them, they all hold on to this simplistic theology. Finally, his friend Elihu takes a more moderate perspective and tries to convince Job that God is the ultimate authority. Job should, in his opinion, focus less on wanting to argue his case before God, and more on surrendering fully to God's will and decisions, knowing that God's infinite wisdom is always just. While Job argues with his other friends, the words of Elihu keep him silent, and hopefully thoughtful enough to be able to listen to a deeper truth.

That truth is expounded upon when God comes and begins speaking to the group. Appearing out of a whirlwind, God reminds Job that he is sovereign and that Job really has no idea about the machinations of the creation of the Universe. Job is not fit to dispute God's actions:

> Where were you when I laid the earth's foundations?
> Speak if you have understanding.
> Do you know who fixed its dimensions
> Or who measured it with a line?
> Onto what were its bases sunk?
> Who set its cornerstone
> When the morning stars sang together
> And all the divine beings shouted for joy? . . .
> Have you ever commanded the day to break,
> Assigned the dawn its place,
> So that it seizes the corners of the earth
> And shakes the wicked out of it? . . .
> If you know of these—tell Me. (Job 38:4-7, 12-13, 18, JPS)

This is just a small part of the speech that God gives to Job, reminding him of the awesomeness that is only God's. Prepared by Elihu's words, Job becomes humbled and finds himself nearly speechless:

> Indeed, I spoke without understanding
> Of things beyond me, which I did not know.
> Hear now, and I will speak;
> I will ask, and You will inform me.
> I had heard You with my ears,
> But now I see You with my eyes;
> Therefore, I recant and relent,
> Being but dust and ashes. (Job 42:3-6, JPS)

God finishes his speaking by chastising Eliphaz, Bildad, and Zophar for their words to Job, which brought him no comfort and mischaracterized God (and mentioning nothing of Elihu, implying that this friend was on the right track). God then restores Job's gifts, even to the extent of doubling what he originally had at the beginning of the book.

While God's interaction with Job toward the closing of the book creates a "happy ending," it still does not help us understand today how we should deal with suffering, other than telling us we should have faith. Before we go into the deeper lessons found in this text about how to deal with suffering, it is worthwhile to examine Job's ultimate reward, and look at some deeper understandings of the results of his journey.

The Hidden Benefits of Suffering: Hitting the Curveball

One of the classic systems of textual analysis is called "gematria." Going back at least to the times of Talmud, this is the correlation of numbers to Hebrew letters and words. Throughout the ages, this has been one of the accepted methodologies of understanding a piece of text at a more subtle and deeper level. This system is often used in conjunction with other Kabbalistic (Jewish mystical) understandings, such as the "Tree of Life," formed of ten energy centers called "Sephirot" (meaning "wheel"). It is through the use of gematria and Kabbalah that we can get an even clearer understanding of how much Job really benefitted in the end, and then begin to examine how Job achieved this beneficial grace.

At the beginning of the book, Job has three daughters, seven sons, seven thousand sheep and goats, three thousand camels, five hundred pairs of cattle, and five hundred asses (Job 1:2-3). At the very end of the story, he is blessed with seven sons and three daughters, fourteen thousand sheep, six thousand camels, one thousand pairs of cattle, and one thousand asses (Job 42:12-13). From a mystical understanding, this is emblematic of a transition from being incomplete to an experience of wholeness.

The ten Sephirot are generally split into two divisions: one of three Sephirot and one of seven. These are the building blocks of all of life, and so from this perspective, Job's possessions are a metaphor for the structure of existence, both on a macrocosmic scale and within his own personal life. The ancient classic text of mysticism *Sefer Yetzirah* ("Book of Formation") teaches that there are twenty-two distinct ways of connecting all these ten points together. If we look at Job's success under the umbrella of this model, we are able to glean more clearly what he really accomplished through his suffering.

At the conclusion of the book, Job has his ten Sephirot back in place as a structure, and is aware of how everything is connected through the twenty-two pathways. How is this seen? The three daughters and seven sons represent the Sephirot, and the twenty-two pathways are seen in the totaling of his possessions (14,000 + 6,000 + 1,000 + 1,000 = 22,000). This is in opposition to Job's understanding of the structure that God created (3 + 7 = 10 children/Sephirot), but only seeing half of what connects everything together at the beginning of his tale (7,000 + 3,000 + 500 + 500 = 11,000). Simply put, in the beginning, Job is a righteous man who knows that God created everything but doesn't experience God in all places, only in the places of good, joy, and righteousness. At the end, he has a personal experience of God not only in the light and easier situations but also in all of creation. Job at the start is aware of how the Universe is structured but not fully conscious of how everything really is connected, and how God is intimately entwined within all of creation. At the end, he experiences Divinity in every aspect of Life. This is what his suffering accomplished: a personal relationship with God in all the aspects and ways, all the highs and lows, of Life.

Think about the following for a moment: If you knew without a shadow of a doubt that your own personal suffering would definitely create benefits that would not only serve you in the physical world but would also allow you to appreciate and experience God in all aspects and places of your life, would you still view it as suffering? Or would you just accept that it's worth it to pay that price now in order to have a life that is so much more full and joyous? For the vast majority of us, when we know that there is a definable and real purpose that our suffering achieves, the suffering per se dissipates and we instead embrace the experience as "paying our dues" to achieve a higher goal.

Parents do this when they raise their children, especially in the first few years when the babies are so needy and totally time consuming that sleep deprivation becomes the norm. Medical students do the same when they spend crazy long hours in residency at hospitals prior to becoming full doctors; and clergy spend years studying so that they can eventually serve as religious leaders for their communities. If we know that a result comes from the difficulties, we usually choose to embrace and surrender to those challenges in order to achieve the goal. In that conscious choice to surrender, we transcend the immediate pain and reframe the experience as one that will help us grow toward our goal.

This is the lesson, and the answer, to be found in the book of Job. Job starts off righteous and wealthy, but not necessarily wise. Throughout the book he suffers because he is convinced that he has done no wrong, and so there is no purpose to his pain. He cannot integrate the idea that he has acted appropriately and is still forced to go through the difficulties that he experiences. He fights it, wanting to prove to God that what is happening to him isn't fair and shouldn't be happening. The text pulls on our own heartstrings as we can all relate to Job in some way through our own pain that was unexplainable at the time. And he is right: there is no cause of punishment.

But, like Job, we are not being "punished." It is the exact opposite. We are being trained so that we can have a deeper relationship with God. It is only after Job hears the words of Elihu and then of God that he chooses to consciously surrender to his experience and stop viewing it as an unfair punishment. As soon as Job sees God in the equation not as fickle but as consistent in God's love for all of creation, he begins to transform. The moment that he makes a choice to let go and recognize that there is more than he can possibly understand, he gets a deeper understanding and experience of God than he could have ever imagined or dreamed of. He not only is aware of God's presence in creation—the ten Sephirot—but also becomes conscious and personally experiences the many pathways that God uses to connect all things (the twenty-two pathways of the Tree of Life). Some are pleasant and some unpleasant, but all are a part of how God interacts in every facet of the world at all times. Through consciously experiencing his suffering, Job's blind faith transforms into a personal relationship and awareness of God's constant presence in everything. His faith has become a true knowing that only comes through experience.

This may seem like an extremely difficult lesson to integrate into our own lives, but we don't all have to go through the afflictions that Job experienced in order to experience God in our relationship with our suffering. Most of us have had bad breakups with partners, where we were sure our partners were our soul mates and couldn't imagine living without them. And most of the time, we find that ultimately it was a really good thing that we didn't stay with them, and often find that years later we are in much healthier and more joyous relationships than we could have imagined. Many of us who have been fired from our jobs may have been devastated at the time, and yet we eventually find other positions that are better for us in many ways, and/or we find that our lives are more whole because of the deepening of relationships with family and friends. The suffering of today may be viewed tomorrow as a great gift in our lives.

The book of Job is a reminder of the gifts we can receive once we let go and surrender our will in favor of God's compassion. Our transformation begins when we accept our suffering, and leads to a profound personal experience of God, which then leads to a deeper joy and connection than we could have envisioned prior.

The book of Job is a beautiful piece of writing in the original Hebrew, and there are many translations that capture Job's feelings of pain, betrayal, suffering, indignant righteousness, surrender, and ultimately joy. But there is a simpler way to use this powerful text.

When you feel as if you are not only in pain but are also genuinely suffering like Job in his process of undeserved pain, take a look at just a few of the passages of this piece of Scripture. Listen to the words of Elihu to his friend, in chapters 32 through 37, and really take the words of God to Job, in chapters 38 to 41, into your heart as if God were saying them directly to you. Then take a look at the first and last paragraphs of the book and see how much Job actually gained through the experience. Realize that once Job became quiet and surrendered, his life became doubly blessed. He may have known of God in his joy, but it was in his darkest moments, and in his surrender to God in that darkness, that he came to truly experience God personally.

As you remember the teachings of Job, it is important to also remember the teachings of Robert Bly, who once taught a group of men in a workshop that "just because the cherry trees blossomed after a blight, let us not attribute the fruit to the blight."[2] Job never glorifies his suffering. He never takes pride in it. He ultimately accepts it and, as a result, grows; but never does he praise it. The book of Job does not recommend that we look for suffering, nor that we extol it. But it is important to always remember that Job is not a book that celebrates martyrdom of any sort. It is much too easy when we are suffering to "bleed" all over everyone we know, as if our suffering is a mark of pride. This is not the lesson of Job and not the pathway to his experience of God. This attitude of being proud of our suffering is also an illustration of arrogance as much as arguing that we know better than God and shouldn't be having the experience in the first place. Letting go and surrendering means just that, and it leads to a true humbling of one's self in the eyes of the Divine. Then we are able to learn, grow, and enjoy.

When that curveball comes at you and you don't know why or what to do with it, open up this beautiful book, which is an illustration and expression of God's love for his creation. It's a story that could have been written by any number of authors, or may even be just a parable. When you are in your own dark night of the soul, take a look at Job and his journey. Remind yourself of God's words, Job's surrender, and the ultimate rewards that came about through that letting go into God's will and becoming truly humble. And then take a look at yourself and your journey, and see what is waiting as you go through the darkness. When we consciously experience this blessing of suffering and being humbled, we find God embracing us with love on the other side.

Notes

1. *Rav Schwab on Iyov* (Brooklyn: Mesorah Publications [ArtScroll], 2005), xviii.

2. "Men and the Life of Desire," 1990, audiotape, Scottish Rite Temple, San Francisco. Robert Bly is a poet, university professor, author, and one of the founders of the "men's movement" in the late twentieth century.

4

Proverbs: Knowing God in the Marketplace

It isn't by getting out of the world that we become enlightened,
but by getting into the world.

—Ken Kesey, *Kesey's Garage Sale*

As a young man (some three thousand years ago), King Solomon, the son of King David, has a life-changing dream. God appears to Solomon in this dream and asks him, "Ask, what shall I grant you?" (1 Kgs 3:6, ArtScroll). The wise Solomon's reply not only becomes the foundation for his entire life and monarchy but is also the traditional reason given for his ability to write three exquisitely beautiful and wise books found in the Tanakh:

> Grant, then, Your servant an understanding mind to judge Your people, to distinguish between good and bad; for who can judge this vast people of Yours? (1 Kgs 3:9, JPS)

God not only grants Solomon (who, legends say, was only twelve years old when he had this dream) his request but even deepens it as a reward for Solomon choosing to ask for something that will benefit his people so greatly:

41

> I now do as you have spoken. I grant you a wise and discerning mind; there has never been anyone like you before, nor will anyone like you arise again. And I also grant you what you did not ask for—both riches and glory all your life—the like of which no king has ever had. (1 Kgs 3:12-13, JPS)

This wisdom is seen through the many actions of Solomon as king: the building of the first Temple, his wise decision-making as king and judge, and his ability to negotiate and have peace with his neighbors, to name just a few. But it becomes manifest just as clearly through the writings he has left us, writings that are such an integral part of the Bible. Specifically, Solomon is credited with having written Song of Songs (*Shir HaShirim*), Proverbs (*Mishlei*), and Ecclesiastes (*Kohelet*). According to Rabbi Yonatan of the Talmudic period, Solomon wrote Song of Songs as a young man, Proverbs in his middle age, and Ecclesiastes in his old age (*Shir HaShirim Rabbah* 1:10). These divinely inspired books define "Wisdom literature." To understand any of them, especially the book of Proverbs, we need to understand the man who wrote them.

King Solomon, the Wisest of Humans

Coming from a family with multiple relationship dysfunctions, Solomon was raised as the successor of David, his father. Solomon had to deal with a brother, Adonijah, who tried to take over the throne and was ultimately put to death for the attempt. He was given the name *Kohelet* from the Hebrew word *kahal*, meaning "to congregate," for his great ability to congregate all the wisdom of the world within himself (thanks to God's blessing above) and to congregate people together to learn his teachings. Along with his wisdom, Solomon also had a level of arrogance that allowed him to specifically violate the laws regarding having many horses and many wives: he had both. Eventually this practice would lead to a weakened kingdom of Judah in Solomon's lifetime, to the splitting of the kingdom into the two nations of Judah and Israel shortly after his death, and to the eventual destruction of the kingdom entirely. (The sages teach that this is proof of the Talmudic dictum from *Succah* 52a, "The greater the [person], the greater his [or her] Evil Inclination" [Soncino].) Solomon's divinely inspired wisdom allowed him to create the first temple, a building his father was never allowed to construct, and pull the very light of God into the structure. This wisdom was codified in his many writings, the most easily understood being the book of Proverbs.

Rav Hamnuna of the Talmud claims that King Solomon composed as many as three thousand proverbs (*Eruvin* 21b). Like the wisdom of any great teacher, these words are practical when understood on a simple level, but simultaneously have double meanings that involve deep mystical truths. Many of the teachings are about ethics, the important values that lead to a fulfilling life, and how to interact in a righteous way in the daily practices of life within your community:

> My son, if sinners entice you, do not yield. (1:10)[1]
>
> Trust in the Lord with all your heart,
> And do not rely on your own understanding. (3:5)
>
> Do not withhold good from one who deserves it
> When you have the power to do it. (3:27)
>
> Do not envy a lawless man,
> Or choose any of his ways. (3:31)
>
> Negligent hands cause poverty,
> But diligent hands enrich. (10:4)
>
> When arrogance appears, disgrace follows. (11:2)
>
> Better a meal of vegetables where there is love
> Than a fattened ox where there is hate. (15:17)
>
> Laziness induces sleep,
> And a negligent person will go hungry. (19:15)
>
> Do not boast of tomorrow,
> For you do not know what the day will bring. (27:1)
>
> A fool vents all his rage, but a wise man calms it down.
>   (29:11, ArtScroll)

A greedy man provokes quarrels,
But he who trusts the LORD shall enjoy prosperity. (28:25)

A man's fears become a trap for him. (29:25)

Each of these quotes demonstrates the style and brilliance of King Solomon's expression. They are simplistic and straightforward, giving sound advice about how to interact with those around you, in your workplace and community. At the same time, they have a deep spiritual wisdom if read through a different lens. Each quote can be read as a guide to a more conscious form of living that includes a direct experience of God. We know that it is a psychological truth that a person's fears end up trapping and confining him or her, and it is just as true that the fears a person has about God push away the direct experience of the Divine. As we learned in Job, a fool may get enraged at God, but a wise person calms down that anger in favor of using the circumstance to deepen one's relationship with the Almighty. We constantly see stories in the news about arrogant and highly successful "leaders" who end up disgracing themselves through their actions. The quote about negligent hands can just as easily be understood to mean that the person who chooses not to study, learn, and grow spiritually will become empty, whereas the individual who struggles with the deeper questions finds a deeper peace. The book of Proverbs is filled with these types of statements: statements that are as true on the more ethereal and spiritual levels as they are in the practical ways.

Many faith traditions teach the following story in one fashion or another: A student goes on a mountaintop and finds enlightenment, and comes to tell his teacher. The teacher tells him that this is terrific, but now he has to practice that enlightenment in the marketplace. It's very easy to be "holy" and "righteous" when you don't interact with anyone, but much more difficult to keep that balance when you are faced with the daily issues of mortgages, car payments, relationship issues, and the like. The book of Proverbs is King Solomon's gift to help us make the awareness of God present in our daily lives, and to use the challenges and experiences of our daily lives to enhance our relationship with God.

Divine Experience of Family

King Solomon realized a truth that many people can still vouch for today: the basis of how we interact within our community is modeled with how we treat our spouses. There is an old adage that if you want to know what type of a teacher, therapist, or religious leader someone really is, look at the relationship the person has with his or her spouse. Working within a community begins first with the community at home: the relationship with a life partner. If a man is grateful for his wife, treasures and respects her, and does what he can to support her knowing that the support she gives to him is infinitely valuable, then there is a good chance that this man is a role model in his community, workplace, and environment.

King Solomon recognized this and ended his book of Proverbs by devoting nearly an entire chapter to the "woman of valor" (31:10-31):

> A woman of valor is a precious find
> Her value is far beyond that of rubies.
> Her husband puts his confidence in her,
> And lacks no good thing.
> She is good to him, never bad,
> All the days of her life.
> She looks for wool and flax,
> And sets her hand to them with a will.
> She is like a merchant fleet,
> Bringing her food from afar.
> She rises while it is still night,
> And supplies provisions for her household,
> The daily fare of her maids.
> She sets her mind on an estate and acquires it;
> She plants a vineyard by her own labors.

She girds herself with strength,
And performs her tasks with vigor.
She sees that her business thrives;
Her lamp never goes out at night.
She sets her hand to the distaff;
Her fingers work the spindle.
She gives generously to the poor;
Her hands are stretched out to the needy.
She is not worried for her household because of snow,
For her whole household is dressed in crimson.
She makes covers for herself;
Her clothing is linen and purple.
Her husband is prominent in the gates,
As he sits among the elders of the land.
She makes cloth and sells it,
And offers a girdle to the merchant.
She is clothed with strength and splendor;
She looks to the future cheerfully.
Her mouth is full of wisdom,
Her tongue with kindly teaching.
She oversees the activities of her household
And never eats the bread of idleness.
Her children declare her happy;
Her husband praises her,
"Many women have done well,
But you surpass them all."
Grace is deceptive,
Beauty is illusory;
It is for her fear of the Lord
That a woman is to be praised.
Extol her for the fruit of her hand,
And let her works praise her in the gates.
    (ArtScroll)

These words are recited by husbands around the world to their wives on every Friday evening as part of the Sabbath celebration in Jewish homes. The recitation of it by husbands to their wives reminds them of the magnificence of these women. Although the language can be interpreted by some, according to today's standards, as being sexist, it represents a gratitude that should be present in all marriages. If only for that one time in a week, the spouses who are so concerned with the issues of bills, job, colleagues, and the like take a few moments to remind each other how wonderful they are; and in that reminding, they remember how much of their lives are dependent on each other's deep support in so many ways. Taking the few minutes and saying these words helps to make the love between the two more conscious, appreciated, and treasured.

King Solomon put these words at the very end of Proverbs as a reminder that to function efficiently and righteously in our communities, we need to act correctly within our most primary of relationships. Reciting it each week helps spouses who may be concerned with business worries to remember what is really important, and makes the love more visible and conscious between the couple. But as with all of King Solomon's proverbs, there can be many meanings and interpretations.

If God is viewed in a feminine way (in Hebrew, the term *Shekhinah* is a reference to the female presence of God in the physical world), this passage can just as easily be understood as a recognition of the value of a conscious relationship with God. It is an affirmation that through God all things come, and that each of our daily practices relies on the Almighty. We need to remember that this beautiful passage is not only true about our spouses but also about life. The clarity of and gratitude for our spousal relationships help us to be more centered in all of our community activities; and the same gratitude and awareness of God's influence help us to be more ethical in our actions on a daily basis.

Surviving the Marketplace in a Healthy Way

It is this passage that may be the most useful on a practical level for helping us to experience God in the marketplace. When you feel as if you are getting caught up in work struggles to the detriment of your marriage, this passage is an anchor to hold you steady in the higher values. Treasure your partner first and foremost, and the successes (and challenges) that come with business in your community become less of a stress. Place the relationship in a higher priority, and joy will follow. Like most clergy, I have been with people in their moments of sickness and death, and there really is a consistency in the saying that people don't wish they had spent more time in the office; they wish they had spent more time with their families. They wish that they had let their spouses know how much they were appreciated and loved. Reciting these verses at least once a week helps keep the higher priorities clear.

This last portion of the book of Proverbs, like all of King Solomon's sayings, has a deeper reminder as well, especially for those who are not married. The collection of teachings begins with, "The fear [awe] of God is the beginning of knowledge" (Prov 1:7, ArtScroll). While the majority of the rest of the book contains teachings that demonstrate what people should and will do when they have that awe, it is the last piece of "Eshet Chayil" that is the great tool to achieve that awe, that foundation, of real knowledge.

Nearly every person gets challenged in one's community. We all are tempted to do things that might serve us in one way but are ultimately detrimental to us in the long term. We all need to have techniques, tools, and personal practices to remind us about what is really important. "Eshet Chayil" is one of the best tools available to help us live a life that includes ethics, successful long-term behavior, and joy. At least once a week, read this passage from the book of Proverbs. View it as a recognition not only of the value of your spouse but also of the involvement of God's relationship to you in all your "practical" endeavors. Like some of the psalms studied earlier, it can be a personal reminder of the imminent nature of the Divine, and specifically the relationship of the Divine in your community and business dealings.

The book of Proverbs is filled with great teachings, but so is *Poor Richard's Almanack*. The difference is that this holy book not only involves practical advice for success in the marketplace but also has the potential of leading a person to a deeper level of success in all of Life. By demonstrating God's involvement in all aspects of communal life, King Solomon guides us to an awareness of the intimate nature of each person's relationship with God—even in the "nonspiritual" world. Through these words of wisdom, we can begin to see and experience God in every aspect of our business life. The mundane becomes sacred; the profane becomes Divine.

Study the words of King Solomon, and let them move through you. Remember his statement at the beginning of the book of Proverbs, about the "awe of God" being the basis of knowledge. Then read the verses of "Eshet Chayil" on a larger scale than just referring to your spouse, but as a teaching about God's involvement in every aspect of your life. Fortified by the knowledge of King Solomon found at both the start and end of this book, allow yourself to turn to any page and read the statements about ethical and wise behavior. By making this a part of your weekly (or even daily) habits, you will start to recognize more and more how God is an intimate part of everything you do; and you will have a more direct experience of your relationship with the Divine in each transaction, phone call, email, and personal interaction.

God is not just found in a synagogue or church, and the book of Proverbs is the ultimate manual to help us be aware of God in the marketplace. Every place, every action, and every challenge in a community, business, or group is an opportunity to deepen our relationship with the Holy in ways that we may not yet realize. King Solomon, the wisest of all men, is our guide. The book of Proverbs is the map.

Note

1. Except where noted, the Scripture quotations in this paragraph are taken from JPS.

5

Ecclesiastes:
How to Find Awe in Every Place

I want to know how God created this world. I am not interested in this or that phenomenon, in the spectrum of this or that element. I want to know His thoughts; the rest are details.

—Albert Einstein

The book of Ecclesiastes, known in Hebrew as *Kohelet* (meaning "community" or "assembled"), is filled with the type of wisdom that can most easily be found in the words of elders who have the experience and understanding that only comes with age. The fact that it is still quoted today by musicians such as The Byrds (in the song "Turn! Turn! Turn!"), movies like *Footloose*, and in nearly every funeral ("A time to be born, and a time to die") is a testament to the value of these words.

Although there is a Talmudic opinion in *Bava Batra* 15a that Hezekiah and his colleagues were the authors of the book, it is traditionally accepted that the actual words are those of King Solomon (and that perhaps Hezekiah wrote them down some three hundred years later). The book begins with its own declaration of authorship: "The words of Kohelet son of David, King in Jerusalem" (1:1, ArtScroll). Given that King Solomon was the only son of David to ever become a king in Jerusalem, the authorship has consistently been attributed to this same man who wrote Proverbs and Song of Songs. As discussed earlier, it has traditionally been taught that King Solomon wrote Song of Songs as a young man, Proverbs in his middle age, and Ecclesiastes as an old man. There are numerous understandings of why he used this name. Rashi (1040–1105) believed that it was because he "assembled" much wisdom, Ibn Ezra (1089–1164) felt it was additionally because these words were said in a public assembly, and many just feel that the name is appropriate as Solomon had the unique gift of creating successful communities and assemblies wherever he went. These understandings are not necessarily in contradiction with each other, and it could be as simple as understanding that King Solomon, through the words in this book of wisdom, demonstrates how all things in life are tied and assembled together. The sacred and profane come together in chapter 2 of the book, where he is clear that he has experienced all of life's material pleasures:

> I bought male and female slaves, and I acquired stewards. I also acquired more cattle, both herds and flocks, than all who were before me in Jerusalem. I further amassed silver and gold and treasures of kings and provinces; and I got myself male and female singers, as well as the luxuries of commoners—coffers and coffers of them. Thus, I gained more wealth than anyone before me in Jerusalem. . . . I withheld from my eyes nothing they asked for, and denied myself no enjoyment; rather, I got enjoyment out of all my wealth. (Eccl 2:7-10, JPS)

Similarly, the famous words of chapter 3 of this book are a collection of "times": a time to do one thing, and a time to do its opposite. Solomon assembles them together into an expression of the needs of all things, feelings, and experiences to be joined. Being born and dying, planting and uprooting, slaying and healing, weeping and laughing, wailing and dancing, silence and speaking, war and peace—these and other opposites are assembled together and accepted as a necessary part of the human experience. These words of wisdom are the result of a lifetime of being able to live fully, and a talent for integrating the disparate aspects of all of Life together:

> To every thing there is a season, and a time to every purpose under the heaven;
> A time to be born, and a time to die; a time to plant, and a time to pluck up that which is planted;
> A time to kill, and a time to heal; a time to break down, and a time to build up;
> A time to weep, and a time to laugh; a time to mourn, and a time to dance;
> A time to cast away stones, and a time to gather stones together; a time to embrace, and a time to refrain from embracing;
> A time to seek, and a time to lose; a time to keep, and a time to cast away;
> A time to rend, and a time to sew; a time to keep silence, and a time to speak;
> A time to love, and a time to hate; a time of war, and a time of peace. (Eccl 3:1-8, ArtScroll)

It may be because of these opposite and seeming contradictions that the book was almost not included as part of the canon: "The Sages wished to hide the Book of Ecclesiastes because its words are self-contradictory, yet why did they not hide it? Because it begins with words of Torah, and it concludes with words of Torah [religious teaching]" (Babylonian Talmud, *Shabbat* 30b, Schottenstein).

This key found in the Talmud, looking at the bookends of the start and finish of this text, provides a greater understanding of the magnificent wisdom of Solomon. Despite the implications that the book is filled with inherent contradictions, there are truths to be found here that help us deepen and become more conscious of our relationship with God in all aspects of Life.

The Depths of Awe Become the Heights of Understanding

The last sentence of Ecclesiastes is a simple example of clearly "religious" writing: "The sum of the matter, when all is considered: have awe of God and protect his commandments, for this is for all mankind" (12:13). This is a straightforward sentence that reminds us that our entire life's duty is to be in awe (as discussed earlier, sometimes translated as "fear," but more appropriately "awe" or "revere") of God, and to protect (or "observe") the commandments. It's a clear theology that is easy to understand but takes a lifetime of practice to embody. If the entire book were this simple, there would undoubtedly have been no Talmudic dialogue about hiding the text.

The first part of Ecclesiastes (after identifying King Solomon as the author) is more difficult, and is among the most commonly misunderstood statements in the entire Bible:

> Futility of futilities, said Kohelet. Futility of futilities. All is futile. What profit does man have for all his labor which he toils beneath the sun? . . . There is nothing new under the sun! (1:2-3, 9, ArtScroll)

Knowing that King Solomon wrote these words as a man approaching his death, these at first seem like words of depression and ennui. These words are often interpreted as the world-weary expressions of an old man who has experienced everything that Life has to offer, and come to the conclusion that everything is meaningless. At first read, it seems as if King Solomon had realized toward the end of his life that everything in this world is a waste of time. Were it not for the statement at the end of the book that reminds us to have awe of God, this entire text might be (and sometimes is) interpreted as an argument made by an old man to not waste any time of our brief lives interacting with the material world. From this perspective, the book of Ecclesiastes seems to be the expression of an old man's existential crisis: a reminder that there is "nothing new under the sun" and a suggestion to focus instead on guarding God's commandments. Sadly, this is how the very uplifting text is all too often viewed, as opposed to looking deeper into what King Solomon, the wisest of men, is really teaching us.

As discussed earlier, Solomon had asked God for a listening, understanding heart in his dream as a young man. His great wisdom, compassion, and empathy were unique in history. If we remember that premise, then it becomes easier to see an interpretation of these opening verses that is more in alignment with the author's beliefs.

No matter how much money we have, we all die without being able to take any of our monetary profits with us. King Solomon had the wisdom to understand that basic truth. The real profit is found in what can be carried within ourselves, both during and after our lives. Again, the sages of the Talmud help us understand these words better. "Only in striving for profit in what is under the sun is there no gain, but in striving for those things which *preceded* the sun [religious understanding], there is profit" (*Shabbat* 30b; Schottenstein, italics mine). The book begins with the deep understanding of King Solomon that there is profit to be made by investing in our spiritual growth: the work we do in that realm "before the sun" is the purpose of Life.

But how does this interpretation integrate with the first phrase of "Futility of futilities. All is futile"? The Ramban (Nachmanides, 1194–1270), among others, defines the Hebrew word *hevel* not as "futility," but as a noticeable mist, a vapor. Using this definition, the opening lines make perfect sense and are not depressing at all. Combining these two understandings, the first lines could be creatively read in a very different way:

> Vapors and mist. Everything in this world is as transient as a mist. All material profits are temporary, and the only real profits are those that help us to experience what existed before this physical world; and what transcends all of the illusions of Life.

Using this interpretation, King Solomon sounds like he is quoting the Buddha about the illusory quality of physical existence. An introductory paragraph with that intention implies that the rest of the book will be about not being attached to the physical world's pleasures and pains. But this wise king teaches the exact opposite throughout the book, and instead of the nonattachment philosophy of Buddhism, King Solomon reminds the reader that he made the choice to experience everything physical that can be found in this world. How can we resolve this recognition of the transitory nature of existence with the rest of the book, which describes the entire physical world in such specific and spectacular terms? In answering that question, we can find the real purpose and intent of this book, how it fits into the entire section of Ketuvim and how we can use it in our daily lives to enhance our awareness of God.

King Solomon gives us a hint of how to understand the depths of this text by the name he uses in the very beginning: Kohelet. "Assembly" or "community." Throughout the book he speaks of all aspects of the physical life: slaves and wives, cattle and palaces, plants and animals—everything that can be found in any part of the world is described or alluded to in the writings. Solomon's name of Kohelet says it all: assemble them. View them as a singular community. See them as an organism that is tied together like a unified field of force. Yes, they are each unique, but they are all connected as well, in the same way that our left and right hands are separate but also part of the same larger being.

But King Solomon in his old age teaches us to do more than just see the connections of everything in life; he asks us to experience the connecting force itself. Be in awe of God, if for no other reason than seeing that everything in life is a reflection of God and has a Divine spark that motivates it. Even though all things physical will eventually blow away like a mist, if we protect the Torah's commandments (which by definition means that we must learn, understand, and observe them), then we can see God in all things around us.

This may seem like a large leap: from seeing the Divinity in all things to protecting the commandments to being in awe. But the pathway of King Solomon as found in Ecclesiastes gives us a road map to make that leap.

Seeing the Divine in Every Place in Every Moment

There is an old folk story told by rabbis throughout the centuries: A young boy was so brilliant and insightful that he was sent to a religious university when he was just a ten-year-old child. Upon arriving there, the older students wanted to make fun of him. So they said, "We'll give you a dollar if you can show us where God is." The wise boy replied, "I'll give you ten dollars if you can show me where he isn't."[1] The book of Ecclesiastes reminds us of the deep wisdom of this boy.

King Solomon describes all the different aspects of life in this text, and tells us to see God in all of them through the guarding of the Torah's commandments. There are 613 laws in the Torah. These laws not only tell us how to deal with other people ethically and compassionately but even describe how we should treat plants and animals. If animals are to be killed, then they are to be killed with compassion; and we are not even supposed to eat the fruits of a tree for the first three years. Over and over, the commandments teach respect for all of Life. Everything is Divine, and the observance of the commandments helps us to remember this basic spiritual truth. As is said in the Sikh tradition and others of India, "Namaste," meaning "the divinity in me recognizes the divinity in you." The book of Ecclesiastes is not only King Solomon's teaching of the Divinity in all things and experiences but also a study guide in how to experience that Divine spark in all of Life.

With all the stresses and responsibilities of living in the twenty-first century, it is easy to forget that everything and everyone is really filled with a Divine spark. When someone cuts us off on the freeway or we get frustrated because things just aren't going the way we wanted, it becomes all too commonplace for us to forget that God is part of every thing and every experience. We get out of balance and forget what the important priorities in life are. Instead of spending time with our children, all too many of us rationalize that it is more important to spend time making profits. King Solomon reminds us that those profits are all temporary and that we need to focus on the more permanent and real truths.

It's ironic how many people go through a midlife crisis when they recognize that what they thought was important really is not. They fill the hours of their lives working to make a financial profit, only to realize that the profit is not what is important and that their lives are empty. King Solomon tells us to be aware of this, to live a life that is filled with the awe of God. An awe that comes about because we remember and experience the Divinity in all things. Try the brief "what if" exercise discussed earlier in the chapter on Psalms: Imagine for a moment—what if . . .? What if every sound, every color, every thing that is around you right now, is a gift from God designed specifically for you right now? What if everything is being choreographed for your soul's benefit? And what if you are part of the Divine choreography and are also a gift to everyone around you? Take a full breath, and with each inhale and exhale, be conscious of every plant, animal, person, and feeling that comes your way, accepting them all as a part of Divinity. For most people, when they really allow themselves to creatively visualize and feel this, they find that they are suddenly filled with a sense of true awe. Put differently, there is a Hasidic teaching that if you treated all people you met as if they were the Messiah, it wouldn't matter if they weren't.[2]

When you feel like you are getting caught up in the daily grind and forgetting the Divinity in all things, open the book of Ecclesiastes. Don't view it as a text of depression, but as a road map that reminds you of all the Divine sparks around you. Open to any page, although the beautiful words of chapter 3 may be the easiest to integrate. Take the words that you read, and see if you can find the Divinity that is hidden within your personal encounter with that experience. Can you experience God in planting and harvesting? in laughter and tears? in birth and in death? Take the words as reminders to yourself to look for God in each experience of the physical world. Recognize the Divine spark that is inside all things. Realize the joy that comes with this feeling, and the sense of awe that follows in the knowing that everything really is a Divine gift. With that awe, you begin to accept the wisdom of King Solomon.

In the Talmudic tractate *Berachot*, it is said that if one sees the book of Ecclesiastes in a dream, "he may hope for wisdom" (57b, Soncino). Let the words help you dream and experience God in all aspects of the physical and sometimes profane world. King Solomon is the great guide to experiencing joy instead of depression, gratitude instead of arrogance, and wisdom instead of folly. Allow his words to lead you to a true sense of awe, and to the recognition of God in everything that you touch and in every face that you see.

Notes

1. Like many folk stories, this is attributed to and adapted by many different rabbis.

2. Ibid. Similarly, there are many Hasidic masters who have been attributed with a version of this teaching.

6

Song of Songs:
Integrating Intimacy and the Divine

The whole world is not as worthy as the day on which the
Song of Songs was given to Israel; for all the Writings are
holy, but the Song of Songs is the Holy of Holies.

—Rabbi Akiva, *Mishnah Yadayim* 3:5

Traditionally viewed as a book of love written by King Solomon
as a young man, Song of Songs (*Shir HaShirim*; also sometimes
called Song of Solomon after its author) is a text that oozes sensuality, intensity, and intimacy in nearly every word. The text is
a dialogue between two lovers expressing their desire for each
other as they progress toward consummating their relationship.
For the last thousand years, it is usually interpreted allegorically,
not as a love sonnet between a man and woman, but as vows and
an expression of the love between God and Israel. But perhaps
with study, we may be able to see that it is both literal and allegori-
cal, and even more than either singular understanding.

The Sensual Union with the Divine

The book starts with an attribution in the first verse of "Song of Songs, that is for Shlomo" (Solomon's Hebrew name; ArtScroll). There are those who believe that Shlomo, which also means "His peace," is a reference that the book is written for God, and even the Talmud makes a reference in *Bava Batra* that Hezekiah is the author of the book (on page 15a, the same place it suggests that Hezekiah also wrote both Proverbs and Ecclesiastes). But the common and traditional opinion in both the Talmud and subsequent commentaries throughout the centuries has been that it was actually written by Solomon. Academics, linguistic experts, and biblical historians have tried to place it anywhere from 900 BCE to the sixth century CE, but even these scholars generally believe that it was based on Solomon's orally transmitted words. Accepting that it is initially (if not literally) the words of Solomon, we are faced with another, greater challenge: the explicit sensuality of the book, and what this implies in terms of it being a sacred text and part of the biblical canon.

> How beautiful are your feet in sandals.
> O Prince's daughter, your rounded thighs are like jewels, the
>   work of the hands of an artist
> Your navel is like a round goblet; that never lacks blended wine
> Your belly is like a heap of wheat set about with lilies
> Your two breasts are like fawns, twins of a gazelle. . . .
>
> May your breasts be like clusters of the vine, and the scent of
>   your breath like apples
> And the roof of your mouth like the best wine for my beloved
> That goes down sweetly, causing the sleeper's lips to murmur
> I am my beloved's and his desire is for me
> Come my beloved, let us go forth into the field.
>   (*Shir HaShirim* 7:2-4, 9-12, ArtScroll)

This is a mild sample compared to some of the explicit words of love expressed in this book written by King Solomon, a man who was later in life to become the husband to a thousand wives.

Before delving deeper into the book and how it can be used, it is important to realize a consistency that is found in the deeply spiritual writings of many of the great mystics throughout the ages from all spiritual traditions. The experience of the mystic, who has a full, direct, and personal experience of unification with God (called *yichud* in Hebrew), is so all-encompassing, so over-whelming, that there is a constant expression of it in terms that sound like the pillow talk of lovers. To recognize that this style of language is common among these enlightened teachers around the world is important, and it's worth taking a brief look at other examples of "love" poetry being descriptive of the Divine:

> O my Beloved
> Take me
> Liberate my soul
> Fill me with Your love
> and release me from all the worlds.
>
> If I set my heart
> On anything but you
> O fire, burn me from inside!
>
> O my Beloved
> Take away what I want
> Take away what I do
> Take away everything
> that takes me from you
> (Rumi, thirteenth-century Sufi mystic)[1]

Love has no other desire but to fulfill itself.
   But if you love and must needs have desires, let these be your desires:
   To melt and be like a running brook that sings its melody to the night.
   To know the pain of too much tenderness.
   To be wounded by your own understanding of love;
   And to bleed willingly and joyfully.
   To wake at dawn with a winged heart and give thanks for another day of loving;

To rest at the noon hour and meditate love's ecstasy;
To return home at eventide with gratitude;
And then to sleep with a prayer for the beloved in your
heart and a song of praise upon your lips.
(*The Prophet* by Kahlil Gibran, an early twentieth-century
Eastern Catholic mystic)[2]

When men bring tribute, an ox, say, or dove,
The lean or the fat gives Thee equal delight,
If but 'tis brought by a heart full of love,
So too take my prayer as priestly rite
For my soul and spirit unite in Thy praise,
Two things having met in me, one in their ways.
(Solomon Ibn Gabirol, eleventh-century Kabbalist)[3]

The idea that the soul will join with the ecstatic
just because the body is rotten—
that is all fantasy.
What is found now is found then.
If you find nothing now,
you will simply end up with an apartment in the City of
Death.
If you make love with the divine now, in the next life you will
have the face of satisfied desire.

So plunge into the truth, find out who the Teacher is, Believe
in the Great Sound!

Kabir says this: When the Guest is being searched for, it is the
intensity of the longing for the Guest that does all the
work.
Look at me, and you will see a slave of that intensity.
(Kabir, fifteenth-century Indian saint [translation by Robert
Bly])[4]

Looking at just these samples, we can see that Solomon's Song of
Songs can have at least a dual meaning of the relationship with a
lover, and/or the relationship with God. But why does Rabbi
Akiva, one of the greatest sages of all time, declare that it is the
holy of holies?

Success, Sensuality, and the Temple

To understand Rabbi Akiva's comment, as well as start to understand how we can use this text to enhance our own lives and relationships with God, we need to know just a bit more about King Solomon. We've already discussed some of his wisdom and history in the chapters dealing with Proverbs and Ecclesiastes. Remember that Solomon was the son of King David, the greatest king of Israel and the ancestor of the Messiah. It was David who wanted to build the holy temple but was prohibited by God, with it ultimately being built by King Solomon. The temple, which (although built by King Solomon) would be known as the house of David and considered the supreme building, was sanctified on the day of its dedication with a psalm of David (Psalm 30 begins with "A Psalm and Song at the Dedication of the House of David" [ArtScroll]). Solomon had started working on the temple in the fourth year of his reign, and it took seven years to be completed. Since he assumed the throne at the age of twelve, we can conclude that the temple was built and dedicated when King Solomon was only twenty-three. It was then, at the prime of his young manhood, that we are traditionally taught that Solomon completed the Song of Songs text. As it says in the *Zohar*, "King Solomon was inspired to compose the Song of Songs when the Holy Temple was built" (*Shir HaShirim*, ArtScroll, xxxii). Rabbi Akiva recognized the holiness of the book, and may even have been comparing it to the holy of holies (the most "sacred" physical part of the temple building) within the temple structure itself when he described Song of Songs. Or Rabbi Akiva may have realized that while the temple was a structure built by man and would eventually be destroyed, King Solomon's most beautiful of songs would last forever and inspire others to find their own holy of holies within themselves as Judaism became a "portable homeland" culture without a central building. But to understand how to use this text, it becomes important to examine Solomon even deeper, as both a wise king and as a young man.

At twenty-three years old, when the temple was completed, King Solomon was truly at the height of glory. According to the Bible, his kingdom was unified and at peace, he had more wisdom than any human being before or since, he was respected by neighboring kingdoms, and he was a young man in the prime of his life in all ways. This moment of the temple was not only the pinnacle of his kingship but also was the realization of his father's dreams. It was as if he had won the Super Bowl, World Series, NBA Championship, and two Nobel prizes all at the same time. At the age of twenty-three.

One of the beautiful aspects of the Tanakh is that our leaders are not Divine; they are human beings. They have human desires, make human mistakes, and redeem themselves. They are not out of the reach of the rest of us, and are models of how we can live if we have the same courage, passion, wisdom, and faith that they exemplified. Solomon was no different.

If any twenty-three-year-old was that successful, or even had just one of those championships, it's a fairly good guess that his libido would be highly active as well. If we're honest, the place that many young people say "Oh God" the most is in the bedroom, when they are making love to their partner. King Solomon would certainly have recognized that fact, if not from personal experience, then from dialogues he would have had with his contemporaries. But since he already had been gifted with the greatest of wisdom, an "understanding heart" (1 Kgs 3:9, ArtScroll), he would know how to take this passion that is found in a young man and use it as a way of being conscious of God.

Sex, Solomon, and Intensity

Sexuality is one of the primary forces of nature. As brief as an orgasm may be, it is so powerful and intense that it can motivate a person in more ways than can be imagined. In search of that sexual pleasure, a person may do things that he or she is not proud of in the light of day and consciousness. The power of sexual desire can be found all around us, throughout the media, in advertising (salespeople know that sex sells), and in every aspect of our lives. No matter how many amazing resources are available on the internet, the pornography sites are still some of the largest and most visited, and many are still the most profitable businesses in that medium.[5] Sex is a powerful urge and, as a result, potentially dangerous. Marriages, cultures, and even entire societies have been destroyed through inappropriate expressions of sexuality. There is one web site that is based entirely on setting up married people for sexual affairs, and out of the millions of web sites available in the world, it is rated in the top 1,000 with over 10 million members. Another adult web site that is geared entirely for pairing couples up for purely sexual encounters is rated in the top 250 sites on the planet with over 30 million members and was sold to a larger corporation in 2007 for 500 million dollars. Clearly, sexual passion is an important part of the human experience.

We are taught that what can damage can also heal, what can destroy can create. Sexuality can destroy things but is as much a potential force for good as it is for destruction. Sexual attraction brings couples together who then make love, have children, raise families, and have lives that bring joy and beauty to the world. The sexual and creative energy known as *Kundalini* in Sanskrit is not only the foundation of physical sexuality but also the force behind the creativity of art, music, and inspiration of all sorts. A part of the Jewish wedding ritual (as well as in other cultures) includes the consummation of the marriage between the bride and groom, known as *yichud* (unification)—the same term that is used to describe the union that the mystic experiences with God, only this time the unification is between the bride and groom. Or is it? Maybe there is more in that moment of *yichud* between a wedding couple that can help us understand the Song of Songs more deeply.

When a couple comes together immediately following their ceremony of marriage under the wedding canopy, the bride and groom traditionally go to a private chamber. The chamber is guarded by a friend or relative (called a *shomer*) outside of their room, who doesn't let anyone disturb the couple. There, in their private chamber, the newly married couple feed each other their favorite foods and drinks, and speak privately for the first time as committed life partners. They also make love, and in that moment, they are embodying the *Ruach HaKodesh* (Sacred Spirit, in masculine form) and the *Shekhinah* (female presence of God), creating a union that affects all of the world. For that brief moment, they are unifying all that is masculine with all that is feminine in a healthy, loving, and passionate way. It is considered part of the ritual of marriage, and most couples speak about it months and years later as the highlight of their wedding day: the moment when they became unified, prior to going out to the chaos of the reception.

This sexual union is clearly sacred. Years ago, Rabbi Larry Goldmark remarked to me that he saw God standing between the bride and groom in a wedding ceremony, tying them together. Most clergy who have officiated many weddings will say the same. There is a sacredness, a holiness, that unifies the bride and groom. This same holiness becomes manifest and enhanced when they come together sexually, with all the intimacy of feeding each other, drinking, and making love together.

This is not just a Jewish concept, and throughout world history there are practices that include sexual union as a spiritual experience, with specific goals of achieving an awareness and experience of Divinity through sexuality. In the Far East and India, there are spiritual traditions in which the couple becomes the physical personification of Shiva and Shakti, male and female deities, respectively. The union of the couple again becomes an opportunity for the human beings to become more aware and engaged with the Divine through the expression of their passion together. From a neurophysiological perspective, we know that an orgasm creates similar brain chemistry to the experience of deep meditation or prayer,[6] again demonstrating that there is and can be a conscious relationship between sexuality and spirituality.

So while Solomon's friends may have been shouting "Oh God!" whenever they had sex, the wisdom of King Solomon realized that there was a deeper truth to their words than they were consciously recognizing. When Solomon had asked God for an "understanding heart," he used the Hebrew word *shomeah*, which not only means "understanding" but is also related to the word *lishmoah*, meaning "to listen." An understanding heart is one that truly listens. Solomon heard the cries and understood that there was a deeper meaning than even the passionate participants realized. He knew that God was present in the act, whether it was an expression of love between the partners, an experience that would lead to the birth of a new life (clearly God is present in transforming the act of sexuality into a pregnancy and child), or even an act of pure passion for pleasure. Solomon understood what sages from around the world have also understood: sexuality can be used as a conscious tool for an expression and experience of Divinity.

While the sexual urge may be primal, a human being may make a conscious choice to use it in a way that adds to life rather than detracts from it, that increases intimacy instead of creating barriers to connection, and that creates and does not destroy. King Solomon knew the potential and power of this desire (he thought that he understood it so well that he would later in his life take seven hundred wives and three hundred concubines, thinking that he would be able to control it). He knew that sexuality could be a powerful tool for experiencing love consciously, not only physically but also spiritually.

Song of Songs is the expression of that wisdom: the understanding that sexuality is not something to be degraded but rather can lift the participants into a conscious awareness of the Divine. It is a double entendre throughout: the passion with your partner becomes a mirror image for the passion that is experienced in a conscious experience and unification with God. This in turn intensifies the physical experience, which like a spiral creates even greater spiritual awareness and intensity. As Kabir said so eloquently, "Look at me, and you will see a slave of that intensity."

Looking through Jewish history, there are traditionally two outstanding moments that are considered to physically demonstrate the Divine love that God has for all of us. The first is the giving of Torah, and God's choice to stay with the Hebrews, hovering between the angels of the cover of the ark that held these commandments: "And you shall put the cover upon the Ark; and in the Ark you shall put the testimony that I shall give you. And there I will meet with you, and I will talk with you from above the cover, from between the two cherubim which are upon the Ark of the Testimony" (Exod 25:21-22, ArtScroll). God demonstrates love by choosing to be accessible during the journey through the desert right above the ark.

The second demonstration of God's great love is the building of the temple. The most important part of the temple was the holy of holies, where the ark (from the desert) was placed. The temple that King Solomon built. The building that was dedicated with a psalm of David, his father, and in which he completed this Song of Songs. Song of Songs becomes King Solomon's verbal expression of the intensity of love not just between people but between God and humans. As my friend Rabbi Steve Robbins has said, "If you think a man can be passionate in his love, think how intense God's love could be if we could really experience it consciously." King Solomon's potent words can guide one into heightened passion with a human, leading to an experience of the Divine in the midst of that physical passion and ultimately to an experience of the passion of Divinity. Solomon knew that when people feel deep love, they respond in kind with their own love and passion, and wrote words that would accomplish that goal, not just with a spouse, but with God.

To Love Another Person Is to See the Face of God

One of the most important and challenging commandments in the Torah to really experience is found in the book of Deuteronomy, 6:5, "You shall love the LORD your God" (JPS). Many people fulfill biblical commandments out of a fear of punishment, but how many are really able to choose to observe them as expressions of the love that they have for the Divine? After all, fearing

God is an easy thing to do; we just have to look at the natural disasters of hurricanes, earthquakes, and the like to experience a fear. Respecting God can be easy as well, when we see the beauty of a sunset or hear the sound of the wind. But loving God?

Even as a young man, King Solomon knew the inherent difficulty in truly loving God. So he couched his goal of helping others both experience God's love and love God within the language of something that was easier to relate to: the eroticism of love between a man and woman. He knew that if this personal physical relationship could be intensified and made conscious, then it could lead to an experience of the deeper love that exists between humans and God. At the heart of the physical building of the temple itself was the holy of holies, and at the heart of the passionate relationship between two people was also a holy of holies: a place of awareness in which we experience the passionate love of a conscious relationship with God.

Sex is all around us in the twenty-first century. We see it everywhere. Our libidos are aroused, our desires moved, and our passion enflamed. Song of Songs is the map to help us channel those energies and desires into an experience of the passion and love of God. There is a commonly told teaching of a man who came to his rabbi and commented that it wasn't appropriate for the rabbi to look at the beautiful young women when they passed by him. The rabbi responded that when he saw beautiful young women, he converted the desire into an appreciation for God, who could create such beauty, and would immediately praise God. The rabbi pointed out that when he saw a beautiful woman, he thought of God, as opposed to the man who thought of women while he was in the synagogue praying. Song of Songs is a handbook to help us transform sexual desire into a love for and with God. King Solomon left all of us a manual to help take sexual relationships to higher levels of intensity, and to transform them into Divine experiences.

Song of Songs is one of the most delicious pieces of writings to read aloud to your sexual partner. On a simple level, it seduces and invites the consummation of the relationship in a physical way. On a deeper level, it simultaneously takes the relationship out of just the physical world and brings an element of spirituality and sacredness to the act. Use it. Receive this gift from Solomon and share it with each other, not only enhancing the intensity of the physical relationship with your partner but also helping to take that relationship and escalate it into an awareness of Divinity.

King Solomon's three books all, in some way, relate to the experience of God's love. Proverbs helps us be conscious of God within the love and relationships that we have in our community. Ecclesiastes guides us to experience God in all places and times. Song of Songs, the holy of holies, allows us to directly know God's love for us, and to feel the passion that comes with that love. Through that passion, we not only feel the passionate caring that God has for us but recognize our own passion and desire to be in unification with the Divine as well. We love God fully.

"You shall love the LORD your God with all your heart and with all your soul and with all your might" (Deut 6:5, JPS; original Hebrew: *V'havta et Adonai Eloheycha b'chol l'vavcha, u'v'chol nafshcha, u'v'chol meodcha.*). Song of Songs, Proverbs, and Ecclesiastes together respectively give us the road map to love God in each of these three ways. *L'vavcha* (your heart) is actually a reference to two hearts (the correct word in Hebrew for "your heart" would be *levcha*, and the double *v* is interpreted as referring to two hearts inside each person), the one with an inclination toward good and the heart that is hidden inside each of us that has an inclination for evil. There is no better piece of writing than Song of Songs to demonstrate how we need to integrate both of the hearts inside us: the heart for good and the one for evil, the one for unbridled lust and the one for committed passion, the heart that is present in the love for another person with the heart that expresses the love between God and man. *Nafshcha* is a word that refers not only to "your soul" but also to the *nefesh*, the specifically physical aspect of the soul. Again, King Solomon gives us the deepest of teachings in the book of Proverbs about how to experience love within the relationship of the physical soul and the community around us.

Meodcha is usually translated as "your might," but again, the subtleties of Hebrew are lost in the translation. The word *meod* means "very," so it is as if we are being told to love God with all our "very-ness," a love with and through all of Life and creation. King Solomon's book of Ecclesiastes guides us in that journey, letting us encounter God in everything, every place, and every time. These three sacred writings guide us into knowing the deeper experience of that primary commandment in Deuteronomy: to love God.

These books are the demonstration that King Solomon really did achieve his wish of having an understanding heart, a heart that listens. Greater even than that wisdom was the kindness of his choice to share it with us, and to guide us to the experiences he knew through the words of each of these powerful and loving texts. May we each receive King Solomon's gift with love, and passionately experience God in all these relationships of the heart, soul, and might.

Notes

1. "The Beloved," in *A Garden Beyond Paradise: The Mystical Poetry of Rumi*, ed. Jonathan Star and Shahram Shiva (New York: Bantam Books, 1992), 4.

2. Kahlil Gibran, *The Prophet* (New York: Alfred A. Knopf, 1945).

3. "Two Things Have Met," in *Selected Religious Poems of Solomon ibn Gabirol*, ed. Israel Davidson (Philadelphia: Jewish Publication Society of America, 1974).

4. *The Kabir Book: Forty-Four of the Ecstatic Poems of Kabir*, ed. Robert Bly (Boston: Beacon Press, 1977), 24–25.

5. So profitable that there is now a .xxx distinction for these types of sites. As an example, numerous sites offering pornography are in the top 500 most visited sites in the world. Statistics found at Alexa: The Web Information Company, http://www.alexa.com.

6. See the work of Eugene G. d'Aquili and Andrew B. Newburg, *The Mystical Mind: Probing the Biology of Religious Experience* (Minneapolis: Fortress Press, 1999), among others, for more information on this topic.

7

Lamentations:
Pain and the Promise That Comes from It

Most great people have attained their greatest success just one step beyond their greatest failure.

—Napoleon Hill, author, advisor to
President Franklin D. Roosevelt, and business philosopher

*Your pain is the breaking of the shell that encloses your
    understanding. . . .
Pain is the bitter potion by which the physician within you
    heals your sick self.*

—Kahlil Gibran, "On Pain," *The Prophet*

Having just finished the three books written by King Solomon, the Ketuvim section continues with the book of Lamentations, the most overtly painful book in the Bible. As we discussed, King Solomon's crowning physical achievement was the creation of the temple. But this building did not last forever, and why it was destroyed, how it was destroyed, and the devastation wreaked afterward are the topics of Lamentations. *Eicha*, the first word and title of the book in Hebrew, translates to "how." As we have often seen, the subtle word choices in these books can lead us to a deeper understanding of their usage. The sages of old discussed whether the title is a reference to the question "*How* could this possibly happen to us?" or, conversely, to the statement "This is *how* it happened." Whether as a question or an answering statement, clearly the book describes the historical nadir of the people up to that time.

Ostensibly, Lamentations is an accounting of a singular event: the destruction of the first temple, which happened on the ninth day of the month of Av in the Hebrew calendar. But what was originally a description of that one horror became a symbol of many more horrors that happened to the Jews on the same date: the destruction of the second temple, the expulsion of the Jews from Spain in 1492, and the beginning of World War I (which directly led to the rise of Hitler and the Holocaust), to name a few.[1] Lamentations has become the text that is the written expression of all great tragedies.

The book of Lamentations is ascribed to the prophet Jeremiah, who lived not only while the first temple was in existence but also through its destruction in the sixth century BCE. Known as the "weeping prophet," Jeremiah is said to have gone to a cave and written down his mourning of the destruction of Jerusalem and the holy temple into a scroll that became the book of Lamentations. He had spent his life chastising and preaching to the Jews while the temple was still standing that if they did not change their idolatrous behavior and practices, God would remove the Divine Presence from them and the temple would be destroyed by enemies. Having spent four decades trying to convince those around him to repent of their ways, it is impossible to conceive of the pain Jeremiah must have felt when his prophecies came true and the temple was destroyed. This painful book is the result of those decades of his pain: the pain of praying that what you foresee will not in fact happen.

The Talmud teaches, "If a person sees that suffering befalls him, let him examine his deeds" (*Berachot* 5a, Schottenstein). Jeremiah had spent his entire life seeing the decay of the society around him, and trying to guide others into once again accepting the ethics and behavior that God had commanded. Although constantly persecuted by everyone around him who did not want to hear his words, he continued to preach this message through the reigns of five kings: Josiah, Jehoahaz, Jehoiakim, Jehoiachin, and Zedekiah. When the destruction finally happened, this man who had been dreading the day of the prophecies was forced to accept the truth that the actions of the people had led to the horrors that he saw. His monumental pain and sadness at the loss of the beautiful temple became the inspiration for the tortured words of the book of Lamentations.

Three prophesied with the expression *Eicha*, "How": Moses, Isaiah, and Jeremiah. Moses said, "How can I alone bear" (Deut 1:12). Isaiah said, "How is the faithful city become a harlot" (Isa 1:21). Jeremiah said, "How! She sits alone" (Lam 1:1).[2] Moses saw Israel in its glory and tranquility, Isaiah saw it in its impetuosity, and Jeremiah saw it in its disgrace (*Eichah Rabbah*).

Biblical commentators throughout the centuries have discussed how each of these men saw a different aspect of Israel. Moses saw her as a maiden who rejected her potential, Isaiah saw her as a harlot who rejected her primary relationship with God in favor of other deities, and Jeremiah saw her as a devastated widow who had lost everything. But what ills could the Jews have done that would possibly justify this complete form of destruction?

> Why was the first Sanctuary destroyed? Because of three [evil] things which prevailed there: idolatry, immorality, bloodshed. . . . But why was the second Sanctuary destroyed, seeing that in its time they were occupying themselves with Torah, [observance of] precepts, and the practice of charity? Because therein prevailed hatred without cause. (*Yoma* 9b, Soncino)

The Talmud explains to us why both temples were destroyed, and gives us warning that if we want to avoid the horrors described in Lamentations, then we need to not only avoid idolatry, immorality, and bloodshed but we also need not have causeless hatred in our lives. It is a simple equation that Jeremiah tried to get the people of his time to understand: if you do certain things that are horrific to your fellow man, then horrific things will ultimately happen to you. This is part of the message of Lamentations: whether we realize it or not, we sow what we reap. The destruction was not undeserved but was the result of the Hebrews' actions. Cause and effect.

No Pain, No Gain

This is the primary difference between the book of Lamentations and the book of Job, where there is no visible cause-and-effect relationship. Suffering is the experience of pain without knowing why. In Lamentations, we learn of the deep pain that happens when we experience the results of our actions: in many ways, a deeper and more painful experience than the experience of existential suffering. It is the expression of the pain of seeing the destruction that is caused by our own earlier actions.

> Jerusalem has greatly sinned,
> Therefore she has become a mockery.
> All who admired her despise her,
> For they have seen her disgraced.
> And she can only sigh
> And shrink back.
> Her uncleanness clings to her skirts. (Lam 1:8-9, ArtScroll)

> The Lord is in the right,
> For I have disobeyed Him.
> Hear, all you peoples,
> And behold my agony:
> My maidens and my youths
> Have gone into captivity!
> I cried out to my friends,
> But they played me false.
> My priests and my elders

Have perished in the city
As they searched for food
To keep themselves alive.
See, O LORD, the distress I am in!
My heart is in anguish,
I know how wrong I was
To disobey.
Outside the sword deals death;
Indoors, the plague. (Lam 1:18-20, JPS)

Little children beg for bread;
None gives them a morsel.
Those who feasted on dainties
Lie famished in the streets;
Those who were reared in purple
Have embraced refuse heaps.
The guilt of my poor people
Exceeded the iniquity of Sodom . . .

With their own hands, tenderhearted women
Have cooked their children;
Such became their fare,
In the disaster of my poor people. (Lam 4:4-6, 10, JPS)

Throughout Lamentations' five chapters, Jeremiah describes in detail the horrors, pain, and suffering of the destruction time, originally called the *Shoah* (a term that was later used as a description for the Holocaust of the twentieth century). He portrays in exquisitely painful detail the suffering of the people for all future generations to hear. Consistently he reminds us throughout the writings that this is "pain," an experience that is a direct result of the actions of the people prior to the destruction. The entire book is a reminder to all people of the future of the depth of pain when we know that we caused it upon ourselves. There is no hiding, no trying to blame anyone or anything else: the pain was foreseen, and is the sum of the actions that went before it.

Isn't this one of the deepest pains people can have? When we are in deep pain, and know that it is because of our own actions? The spouse who experiences the terrible pains of a divorce that was prompted by his infidelity; the businessperson whose poor ethics and subtle thievery lead to an investigation and imprisonment by the government for fraud; the young student who is expelled from graduate school because of her violation of the school's honor code. These are all examples of deep pain that we inflict on ourselves through our own actions. In the daylight of our suffering, we even wonder how we could have gotten to the point of doing those initial actions that caused this pain.

Like an addiction, bad behavior becomes a habit. "If someone commits a sin and then repeats it, he begins to consider it like a permitted act" (Talmud, *Yoma* 86b, Schottenstein). It's the way our psyches work as human beings. As a rabbi, I have been involved in counseling many couples who are considering divorce. There is a pattern if the problems in the relationship were based on infidelity. The first time that the husband or wife has an extramarital affair, he or she feels guilty even while having physical pleasure. The second time, there is less guilt. By the third or fourth time, he or she is only aware of the pleasure. By the fifth or tenth experience, often it has been justified in his or her mind as being a legitimate form of behavior, rationalizing that it doesn't hurt anyone, or it is needed to keep a spark in the marriage, or even that it is a benefit to his or her spouse. We rationalize away the guilt, and the mistake becomes permitted and even admirable in our eyes. It's the same with the person who cheats on his taxes and justifies it, and then continues to do it at a higher and higher level, rationalizing that the government shouldn't be taxing that much; and then suddenly one year is being audited by the IRS. We allow ourselves to justify what we do, even if we know the first time we do it that it is wrong.

The severe pain comes when we are forced to make restitution for what we have done. It can be so devastating that it shakes us to the very core of our souls, and the guilt and pain combine into a deep shame that makes us think that we can never recover in any way.

How do we move on from there? How can we possibly continue to live in any way that even resembles joy when our lives have been damaged or even destroyed as a result of our own mistakes?

Teshuvah: A Map to Pass through the Dark Night

Again, the book of Lamentations along with commentaries gives us a model out of the dark chasm of our pain:

> But this do I call to mind,
> Therefore I have hope:
> The kindness of the LORD has not ended,
> His mercies are not spent.
> They are renewed every morning—
> Ample is Your grace!
> "The LORD is my portion," I say with full heart;
> Therefore will I hope in Him.
>
> For the Lord does not
> Reject forever,
> But first afflicts, then pardons
> In His abundant kindness.
> For He does not willfully bring grief
> Or affliction to man. (Lam 3:21-24, 31-33, JPS)

When there is affliction, even when it is deserved, the text reminds us that there is hope. Like a parent who chastises a child for the child's own benefit, Jeremiah reminds us that the distress we are experiencing is not making God happy, and that God is committed to making things better for us in the future. Each morning's sunrise is a visible demonstration of the Divine love that exists for us if we are willing to let ourselves be embraced by it. The first step to getting out of the pain that we have caused is to recognize that God too wants us to heal, renew, and be whole and happy. One of the underlying teachings of Jeremiah in this excruciatingly painful text is that there is always a hope that there will be a renewal. A piece of writing from the Talmud continues this thesis even further:

> Rabbi Gamaliel, Rabbi Eleazar ben Azariah, Rabbi Yehoshua, and Rabbi Akiva were coming up to Jerusalem together, and just as they came to the Temple mount they saw a fox emerging from the house of the Holy of Holies. They fell weeping

and Rabbi Akiva laughed. . . . [In explanation when asked about his laughter:] I will take to me faithful witnesses to record Uriah the Priest and Zechariah. . . . [Akiva continued:] So long as Uriah's prophecy had not had its fulfillment [Uriah prophesied that Zion would be ploughed like a field] I had misgivings lest Zechariah's prophecy might not be fulfilled [Zechariah prophesied that old men and old women shall sit in the broad places of Jerusalem]. Now that Uriah's prophecy has been literally fulfilled, it is quite certain that Zechariah's prophesy is also to find its literal fulfillment. Said they to him, "Akiva, you have comforted us!" (*Makkot* 24b, Schottenstein)

When Rabbi Akiva saw that Uriah's prophecy had come true with the lands of the temple becoming a place of fields with foxes, he knew that the other great prophecy about that same land would also come true: the prophecy of Zechariah regarding that it would eventually be a place of old men and women enjoying themselves. Akiva understood that the confirmation of the pain was also a confirmation of the validity of hope for a new beginning. As the eleventh-century text *Midrash Tehillim* notes, "Had I not fallen, I could not have arisen. Had I not sat in the darkness, He would not have been a light for me." Jeremiah's book of Lamentations is a reminder that in the midst of our guilt, blame, shame, and pain we are to have even deeper confidence that there will be redemption. But again, the question must be asked: How do we get to that redemptive place? What do we need to do to get out of the pain?

A few years ago, there was a wonderful Canadian television series titled *Being Erica*. The premise of the story was that Erica, a young single woman who was unhappy, was given the blessing to be able to fix the regrets that she had in her life. She would go back in time, fix them, and then start to see the benefits in her life back in the present. It was sort of a time-traveling/self-help/therapy show. With the help of a special "therapist/angel/doctor," she recognized what her pain really was, the action that had caused it, and then went back and made it right. While we cannot go back in time to fix our regrets when we see their results of pain, there is a process that can start the renewal and healing of our pain, and transform it into the joy that Akiva feels. In the Jewish tradition, that process is called *teshuvah* ("return" or "reconciliation"). Although this process is commonly looked at with regard to sins we have committed against others, on a deeper level it is the perfect process to begin to relieve ourselves of the pain we have caused in our own life.

As difficult as it may be to practice, the process is relatively simple: We need to recognize what we have done wrong. We need to take responsibility and apologize to whomever we have done the wrong to. We then need to make amends, restitution for what we did wrong. The next step is to make a commitment not to do the same error again and then, when the opportunity comes up, to not do it. Although much more ancient, this is similar to the ninth step of any modern twelve-step program: "make direct amends." We need to own what we have done that put us in this place of pain and truly fix it. As difficult as this can be, it is much simpler when we recognize the truth found in Jeremiah's writings, as well as the commentators: God is in the midst of our pain, and wants to help us change for the better.

Lamentations is descriptive writing designed to help us recognize the real ugliness, destruction, and horrors that come about as a result of our own misguided actions. It is the guidebook to let us know that there is hope for the pain to end, and for joy to replace it, if only we are willing to fix the problems that caused the suffering in the first place. Jeremiah knows that if we take the first steps, then we will receive Divine help in our journey out of the pain, through hope, and into joy. As is said on the Jewish holiday of Yom Kippur, "God says to the sinner that if you open the gates of repentance as wide as the head of a needle, then I [meaning God] will force it open wide enough to drive horses through" (*Shir HaShirim Rabbah* 5:22).

Hopefully, few of us will ever have to face the horrors that Jeremiah wrote about so explicitly. Our pains may be just as deep personally, but it is, again thank God, rare for an entire culture to experience a Shoah. But whether it is on a personal level or cultural, Lamentations reminds us to recognize and take responsibility for the cause of our own pain. Then, and only then, can we begin the process of healing from the destructive results that we have caused in our own life.

As hard as it was for Job to recognize God's presence in the midst of his suffering, it is in many ways more difficult for a person to experience God in the middle of pain that he brought on to himself, and to honestly take personal responsibility. Jeremiah gives us a helpful technique in the structure of the book's first four of the five chapters. Each of these chapters is written as acrostics (the first verse beginning with the letter *A*, the second with the letter *B*, etc.). Jeremiah wanted future generations to remember that the roots of our pain are so many that they literally can begin with each letter of the alphabet. And this is a good starting point to begin to get out of the horrors that we inflict upon ourselves.

When the world around you seems as if it is crumbling, take an honest look at yourself, your patterns, and your way of life. Take an inventory of who you are and what you have done that has led you to this painful place in life. Emulate Jeremiah, and write down an alphabetical list of twenty-six things that you have done, thought, acted on, or experienced that are underlying causes of the pain, being brutally honest about yourself. Let each letter be a gateway to your opening and taking responsibility for what you have done to get to this painful place in life. Make a conscious choice to shift the *"How* did I get here?" to "This is *how* I got here."

This in itself is incredibly difficult and can easily lead to even greater depression. Again, look to Jeremiah for help in having hope. Reread the verses cited above from the third chapter of Lamentations, along with the Talmudic teaching of Rabbi Akiva. Remember that after Jeremiah wrote the book of Lamentations commemorating the destruction of the first temple, a second temple was built years later. Although that too was ultimately destroyed, after almost two thousand years Israel became a full nation again in 1948, with the ability to pray at what is left of that second temple. Each time it seems as if taking responsibility for your errors will be overwhelming, remind yourself that God is present with you in your pain, and that the pain is actually a sacred form of guidance to help you achieve a greater joy than you can realize. Like an athletic coach who gives obstacles to make you stronger, God too is cheering for you and helping you in the process of becoming more whole and joyous in a deep way.

Take that hope and awareness of God's presence in your pain, and use it to help you make *teshuvah* for each of the alphabetical items you listed. Truly make amends to the best of your ability. At first, this may be even more painful than the circumstance that brought you to the point of doing this exercise, but persist and make it through. As you do this, you will find two things happen to yourself. You will find it easier and easier to make those difficult amends, and begin to experience that God is present with you in your *teshuvah*. And you will also start to experience a sense of support, as if Life itself is trying to help you in the process to get out of your pain. In Jeremiah's language, this is your experience of the presence of God existing in your pain.

If you ever look in the eyes of a hard-core addict who has been sober for decades, you will see a wisdom and gratitude in his or her very soul. This person has become grateful for the addiction that destroyed his or her life because in the healing of it a true life was found. This, too, is the lesson of Lamentations. Be willing to go into the depths of your pain, and know that you will come out the other side in a better way: more whole, aware, grateful, and peaceful.

Jeremiah's book of Lamentations is brutally honest and, as a result, incredibly painful. Life for each of us also has the possibility of becoming painful, and we too have the opportunity to use that pain to achieve great things. It can be humbling, but owning what we have done in our own lives that led to the deep pain is the first step of healing it. Lamentations, although extreme, is the model for dealing with all of our personal pain.

With the courage and honesty of Jeremiah, and the help of the Divine, the pain becomes a sacred tool that awakens us to God's presence in the darkest moments of our lives. The book of Lamentations is the instrument to help in that journey of embracing the "bitter potion," and awakening to a renewed experience of healing, wholeness, and joy.

Notes

1. This is considered the saddest date in the Jewish calendar. Additionally on the ninth of Av, the spies into Canaan came back without faith; the Bar Kochba Rebellion was put down in 132 CE; the first Crusade was declared in 1095; the Jews were expelled from England in 1290; and the deportation of Jews from the Warsaw ghetto into the concentration camp of Treblinka in 1942 all took place.

2. The Scripture quotations in this paragraph are taken from ArtScroll.

8

Daniel: Time, Timelessness, and the Art of Being Present

And God said to him, "Abraham," and he said, "Hineni"
("I am present").

—Genesis 22:1

Listen Israel, the Lord is God, the Lord is One.

—Deuteronomy 6:4

Hineni. One of the most important Hebrew words found in the Bible. Often translated as "I am present" or "Here I am," *Hineni* is the response given to God by multiple leaders in the Bible. It is infinitely more than a statement of physical location, but is an expression on the part of the speaker that says he knows where he stands and has the courage, willingness, and ability to express it. His soul itself is fully present in all ways, and in so being is able to hear the call of God. It is the Buddhist idea of "mindfulness" verbally expressed, and is one of the most difficult concepts in the world: to be so totally present and aware of the moment that all of time becomes timeless.

The book of Daniel delves into this very difficult issue. Daniel is arguably the most challenging book in the Bible to understand

and interpret, both for theologians and for academics. The religious commentators are forced to deal with detailed and bizarre prophecies (including, among others, visions of an idol made of four metals, a tree that predicts insanity, four great beasts, battling angels, and descriptions of the dead being raised); and the academics can't agree on much of anything in this book regarding its history or structure. But, as we will see as we begin to explore this amazing book, Daniel can be used to more consciously experience God in the construct of time that we live in.

Similar to some of the other great stories related in the Bible, the book of Daniel chronicles another "journey of the hero" from a displaced youth to a great leader. King Nebuchadnezzar of Babylon takes four young Hebrews back home as captives shortly before the destruction of the temple in 587 BCE. Like many shrewd conquerors, he knows that if he takes the best and the brightest young people away from their homes and culture to be raised in another country, it will decrease the chances of a future rebellion. Daniel, Hananiah, Mishael, and Azariah are taken because they are "from the children of Israel, from the royal seed, and from noble youths in whom there was no blemish; good looking, skillful in all wisdom, discriminating in knowledge, and perceptive in learning, and who had the stamina to stand in the king's palace; and to teach them the script and language of the Chaldeans" (Dan 1:3-4, ArtScroll).

They are given Chaldean names—Belteshazzar, Shadrach, Meshach, and Abed-nego, respectively—and are to eat, drink, and learn in the palace. Daniel refuses and convinces the king to let them keep their laws of kashrut ("fit" eating habits required of Jews that prohibit the consumption of certain foods). He immediately defines himself as one who is not only committed to his culture's traditions but conscious of even the most basic practice of eating and drinking.

Daniel is subsequently thrown into a lion's den while he serves under King Darius, and survives in a fashion that is still immortalized in stories, film, and song.

Then the king commanded, and they brought Daniel, and threw him into the den of lions. Now the king spoke and said to Daniel, Your God whom you serve continually, he will save you. And a stone was brought, and laid upon the mouth of the den; and the king sealed it with his own signet, and with the signet of his lords; that nothing might be changed concerning Daniel. Then the king went to his palace, and passed the night fasting; nor were instruments of music brought before him; and his sleep left him. Then the king arose very early in the morning, and went in haste to the den of lions. And when he came to the den, he cried in an anguished voice to Daniel; and the king spoke and said to Daniel, O Daniel, servant of the living God, is your God, whom you serve continually, able to save you from the lions? Then said Daniel to the king, O king, live forever. My God has sent his angel, and has shut the lions' mouths, so that they have not hurt me; because I was found innocent before him; and also before you, O king, have I done no wrong. Then was the king exceedingly glad for him, and commanded that Daniel should be taken up out of the den. So Daniel was taken up out of the den, and no kind of hurt was found upon him, because he believed in his God. (Dan 6:17-24, ArtScroll)

The majority of the remainder of the book is filled with different prophecies about the future of the kingdoms in the area, as well as veiled commentaries and visions about the future coming of the Messiah. Like his ancestor Joseph, Daniel journeys through life as a dream interpreter and a man of visions. In the entirety of the Bible, only these two men are seen as accurate dream interpreters, and both interpret for a king of a foreign nation. The king has a dream that cannot be interpreted, Daniel interprets it accurately, and he rises to become a minister of the king (again, similar to Joseph). The next dramatic moment happens when Daniel's three friends are thrown into a furnace and are able to stay alive with the help of an angel that is seen inside the furnace with them (3:12-26). Daniel is eventually summoned to interpret another dream of the king, who, as Daniel prophesied, goes crazy for seven years before returning to his rule.

This is a disjointed book that deals with so many images and visions, but is at its core a text that follows the journey of a young man through the rulers, rites of passage, dreams, and detailed images of his predictions for the future. But the theme that connects all the different parts can be expressed in one word: time.

Difficulties in Daniel

Even biblical scholars are unable to agree on the structure or history of the book of Daniel. While the book itself seems to have been written immediately after Daniel's public experiences, most linguistic scholars believe that it was written four hundred years later. This is because of several reasons: the text is in both Hebrew and Aramaic; the eight copies of the book that were found as part of the Dead Sea Scrolls (and seem to have been written from the early second century BCE to the first century CE, shortly after the death of Jesus); the inclusion of Greek words in some early copies of the text; and then even more contention due to the inclusion of ancient Persian words in some copies. Simply put, biblical scholars do not have the ability to clearly pin down the time that the book was written in, which seems only appropriate for this book that deals with time itself.

Of all the visions and prophecies that are included in this book, it is the imagery of the end of days and the coming of the Messiah that has intrigued people the most. Whether the book is looked at as a prediction for the coming (and second coming) of Jesus, or as the first coming of the Messiah and messianic times, the book makes it clear that Daniel is taught by the angels about the time of "the end," including the theology of raising the dead when the Messiah comes. It makes it equally clear that Daniel is not to share this information in anything other than a veiled way:

> And at that time there will stand Michael, the great heavenly prince, who stands in support of the children of your people, and there shall be a time of trouble such as never was since

there was a nation till that time. At that time your people will escape, everything that is found written in the book will occur. Many of those who sleep in the dusty earth shall awaken, these for everlasting life, and these for shame, for everlasting abhorrence. And the wise will shine like the radiance of the firmament, and those who make the many righteous, like the stars, forever and ever. As for you, Daniel, obscure the matters and seal the book until the time of the End, let many muse and let knowledge increase. (Dan 12:1-4, ArtScroll)

The deepest questions that humans have about the future and the nature of time itself are explored in the text through Daniel's many experiences. What does the future really bring? What will ultimately happen to the world? Is God really involved in our lives? What happens to us when we die? The primal questions that humans have always asked about the future are investigated through Daniel's many miraculous experiences and visions.

And yet, Daniel is not considered a prophet per se.[1] Referring to an experience Daniel had of seeing the angel Gabriel (Dan 10:7), in which he alone of the people who were with him saw the vision, we are taught in the Talmud, "Haggai, Zechariah, and Malachi. They were superior to him [Daniel] in one way, and he was superior to them in another. They were superior to him because they were Prophets and he was not a Prophet. He was superior to them because he saw and they did not see" (*Megillah* 3a, Schottenstein). The book of Daniel, which includes more prophetic experiences and interpretations than most books in the Bible, is not included in the Prophets (Neviʾim) section of the Bible, and Daniel himself is explicitly not considered a prophet by the sages of the Talmud. This simple fact of where it is placed in the canon and how he was viewed by the Talmudic sages demonstrates that there may be a deeper lesson to learn from this book than prophetic visions.

The seemingly unanswerable questions about the future are answered in this book, but are veiled and obscured by the explicit direction of angels to Daniel. The book of Daniel is not to give us a timetable about the future, nor to only elucidate a historical past.

Daniel teaches us how to be so present and aware of "the now" that past, present, and future are more integrated.

The name Daniel in Hebrew translates to "my judgment is God's." It is an expression that reminds the reader that all things rest in God's dominion. "Everything is in the hands of heaven except the fear [awe] of heaven" (Talmud, *Berachot* 33b, Soncino). Although there are pages of discussion in the Talmud in the tractate *Sanhedrin* about when the Messiah will come, it also explicitly says, "Blasted be the bones of those who calculate the end" (*Sanhedrin* 97b, Soncino). Daniel may be given information, but he makes it obscure because he knows that everything is God's judgment. Despite what he sees in his visions, it is through the experience of God that one can even have a glimmer of real truth and timing. Daniel's name is the perfect reflection of his actions. No matter what the circumstance that Daniel experiences, he maintains a consistent pattern of being present and aware of God's direct interaction with all of Life, giving it much more importance than anything that he experiences with a physical, secular king.

Most people worry about the future, especially if they have children. Caring people the world over ask the question, What will the world be like for future generations? Will a messianic time of peace come, or will the world destroy itself through man-made disasters? There are entire denominations of Christianity that are devoted to determining and being part of the "end times." The book of Daniel explicitly states that Daniel knows the answers to these questions, and the interpretations of his visions can be used by any philosophy or individual who is trying to find an answer based on the text.

Perhaps the real answer of Daniel is not found in the detailed (and sometimes bizarre) visions. Maybe the deeper response is not to try to interpret the text's descriptions, but instead to model the behavior of Daniel in a way that allows each individual to have an understanding of these issues through one's own experience.

Do You Have the Time?

Before delving deeper into what can be learned from Daniel, it would be good to recognize the spiritual realities of "time." Most spiritual traditions speak of past, present, and future as being integrated; and there is the great paradox that (a) everything is destined, and (b) we all have free will. The resolution of these conflicting statements is described in many mystical traditions by becoming so aware of the here and now, that all time and place become woven together into a personal "spiritual" experience and that time itself is relative to what we are experiencing in the moment. This may at first sound weird, but most of us have had those moments of time slowing down or speeding up in one way or another.

Ten seconds is an incredibly short period of time when we are on the phone, working in an office, or driving in traffic. But for the athlete running the hundred-yard dash in a race, it seems long as each breath and every movement seem to be lengthened. The personal experience of the ten seconds for the athlete is much longer than ten seconds spent in a classroom or office. Similarly, the ten-second kiss at a wedding seems so short, but is the same amount of time "objectively" that was spent running a hundred yards. Time is relative. We all experience it in some way. Five minutes waiting in the dentist's office or in line may seem like forever, while five minutes of playing basketball with our children goes by so quickly. We may be asleep for only ten minutes, but in that time have had a dream where we feel as if we lived a lifetime. Although the clock is objective, the experience is subjective.

The primal experiences of passion/excitement, terror/fear, and rage/anger all radically affect how we experience moments in time. Our personal experiences are based on our relationship with what we are doing much more than they are based on the clock on the wall. When we are deeply involved with something, time becomes "timeless," and the clock becomes inconsequential to our experience. But how can we consciously step into that timeless quality, and what can happen when we do?

Most competitive athletes have experienced being "in the zone," the term that is used to describe an athlete's experience when everything flows together absolutely perfectly. It is that moment when he knows the ball is going in the basket and doesn't even need to look; when she knows that her golf swing will be perfect and for those few holes she will shoot par—when everything is just perfect. All the hours of preparation and workouts come together with ease and effortlessness as he or she is so present in the very moment, aware of the nearly automatic success that will follow. This is "the zone" that athletes try to experience consciously to enhance their performance on the field. It is also the perfect description of *Hineni*, of being fully present in the moment.

Try something for a moment. Take a deep breath, and exhale it fully. Now, as you continue breathing, try to find the moment where the breath becomes yours. Before you inhale, the air is around you: it is part of the room. When you exhale, it is your breath that you are exhaling (if you have eaten garlic pizza, as an example, it is clear to everyone that it is your breath). As you are inhaling, try to find the moment when the breath from outside becomes yours. When you think you have found the moment, try to find the millisecond. When you've found the millisecond, try to find the microsecond. Try to be aware of the infinitely small moment where the breath becomes yours as the air moves in and out of you. Do this for a few breaths right now.

As you tried to find the infinitely small place of transition, do you notice that your senses are more acute? Most people find in doing this exercise that their peripheral vision is extended, or their hearing a bit more sensitive to the sounds around them. Like the old meditation of contemplating the exact moment when a seed becomes a plant, this exercise is a simple way to sharpen your awareness and consciousness of this very moment. Notice something else as well: the "objective" time of your breathing did not change, but your experience of the breath itself did. You stepped from "time" into "timelessness" by becoming more aware of the moment itself. What does this have to do with Daniel?

Fears are based on what our minds project about the future based on what has been experienced in the past. We were hurt emotionally by someone years ago, and so we are scared to be emotionally vulnerable with someone new. We were hurt while riding a horse, and so we are hesitant to get back on the horse for fear that we will be hurt again. *Fears are the mind's way of protecting us based on past experiences.* In other words, fear is never found while being present in the here and now. When we are fully present, then there is no fear because there is no projection from our minds based on the past.

The book of Daniel deals with macrocosmic issues. It explores the fears that are experienced by both individuals personally and entire cultures collectively. Will our country be safe in the next decade? What will happen to our family in the future? What happens after we die? Will this world destroy itself, or bring itself to peace? Daniel's prophecies and dream interpretations deal with these very great and intimate concerns. The future of the Babylonian, Hebrew, Greek, and Roman kingdoms are all included as part of his interpretations. The raising of the dead, the coming of the Messiah, and the end times that accompany the process are all alluded to in the text. While Daniel may be vague in his visions, the text does imply what allows him to be so present that he is aware of the future.

When Daniel first comes to the court of Nebuchadnezzar, he refuses to eat the forbidden food. He suggests instead to the king that he and his three friends eat only legumes and water for ten days to see how they do. At the end of the ten days, it is clear to the king that they were healthier than all the other youths who were eating the king's food (1:12). Daniel sticks to his beliefs, and acts upon them. He continues the process when he is thrown into the lions' den to be killed. Despite any fear that being in a den of lions may cause, he trusts in God and prays, and survives the night (6:24). Again, he goes to his roots of prayer and trust and is unharmed. Before his dream of four beasts representing four kingdoms, Daniel was upon his bed (7:1), the place where, as an observant Jew, he would have had his evening meditations and prayers. Before his prophecy of the seventy weeks and coming of the Messiah, Daniel "turned" his face toward God, "devoting [him]self to prayer and supplication, in fasting, in sackcloth and ashes" (9:3, JPS). Again, he makes a conscious effort to step out of the requirements of his physical body in preference of turning toward an awareness of God.

Daniel gives us a model for being aware of God in our relationship with time and the future, by showing us that we need to step into "timelessness." In so doing, we become aware of the future without a fear, or at least become comfortable with it. The huge questions about the future, like what will happen after we die, become either answered or may even become unimportant to us as we live in the present moment. Daniel achieves this level of presence, of *Hineni*, through the rituals of his culture and religion: eating practices, meditation, prayer, fasting, and using sackcloth and ashes. This is the key to understanding what we dream, how we interpret the future, and how we bring a period of peace into the world: being present.

We all have our own tools to help us become present, to say "*Hineni.*" They may be personal, rooted in our experiences with family and friends, or may come from the culture in which we grew up. When we have concerns about those macrocosmic issues of death, afterlife, survival of our culture in the future, and the like, we need to use those tools to be more present in the "now," and as a direct result let those concerns dissipate and dissolve.

Often these fears come up when we are faced with numinous moments: confrontations that come up as life-cycle moments. As a rabbi, I have been honored to participate in the mourning and burial processes for many people, a time when these macro-concerns often become conscious for the survivors of the deceased. In Judaism, there is a traditional process of mourning that involves the mourners holding services in their home for a week (and continuing on for the rest of the month at services at a synagogue), studying text in honor of the deceased, and other practices such as not cutting hair. Sadly, for many secular Jews, these practices are considered archaic and have no meaning to them. I consistently make it a point to explain to the family that these practices accomplish two goals: the soul of the departed will be elevated by their prayers and study, and they will mark the time of the first week (and month) of missing their loved one in a conscious way. Still, often families do not want to observe these practices. So I developed a different answer that, while not being observant in a traditional way, gives them the opportunity to be a bit more conscious in their mourning.[2]

I suggest to families to learn something every day in honor of their loved one. Whether it is French or flute, Spanish or saxophone, my suggestion is to take a little bit of time each day to learn something in their loved one's honor. This will accomplish a few things. It will give the soul of the departed joy, for it always makes us happy when someone we love learns something new in our honor. As importantly, it will help the mourner mark the time consciously. If the mourner had lunch with his mother every Sunday, this learning will help him heal on that first Sunday without her. Additionally, the rest of his life, whenever he speaks Spanish or plays the flute, he will think of her with joy, and again the healing will be increased. No longer will he worry so much about the future but instead be present in the moment of both his grief and choice to continue on with growing his own life. While this is not a traditional mourning practice, countless families have thanked me for it afterward, as it helped them deal with both the personal loss and the existential fears that arose because of the confrontation with their own mortality.

This is what Daniel teaches us to do: to make a choice to be present through ritual, meditation, prayer, or any effective personal practice to understand and integrate the future with the present. For centuries, wise scholars and sages have attempted to decipher the visions and dreams of Daniel in order to understand the future more clearly. But most of us have neither the time nor the self-discipline to spend the thousands of hours tearing apart the text in that way. More practically, the book of Daniel is a teaching that if we prepare ourselves through personal rituals, we can be aware of the future without fearing it. By being present, we can integrate the world around us in vast permutations through making a conscious effort to deepen our relationship with the Divine.

The Future Is Now

When you have a fear of the future, or a concern for those macrocosmic issues, look at the book of Daniel as a model. Like Daniel, make a conscious choice to turn yourself to God and listen. Yogi Bhajan Khalsa, one of the great teachers of meditation and yoga of the twentieth century and the founder of the Sikh movement in the West, was fond of saying, "Prayer is when the mind is one pointed and man talks to Infinity. Meditation is when the mind becomes totally clean and receptive, and Infinity talks to man."[3]

Find your own personal form of meditation, and listen to the Infinite. Whether it is a ritual that involves fasting, proper eating, dress, or any form of cultural ceremony that you are comfortable with, use it as a way of listening. Like Daniel, become a vessel that can receive, and use your own techniques to accomplish that in a way that works for you. Read the story of Daniel in the lions' den (chap. 6), and try to creatively visualize yourself in that den instead of Daniel. How do you feel? What do you do to center yourself in that moment of terror surrounded by lions? Meditate. Breathe. Listen.

When Life presents us with the concerns of the future, for whatever reason (the birth of a new child causes this as deeply as the death of a loved one), we need to take moments for ourselves to listen to the deeper presence of God in the midst of those moments. Before we can respond, "*Hineni,* I am present," we must hear the calling of Life asking for us.

The prayer known as the Shema is often called the watchword of the Jewish faith, and is usually translated similarly to the quote at the beginning of this chapter. But Rabbi Stan Levy has another wonderful way of interpreting it that is very much in harmony with the preparations of Daniel before each of his experiences: "Listen, you who wrestle with God. The God outside you and the God inside you are the same." When, through meditation or other rituals, we are able to listen to the Infinite and really recognize that all things are connected, when we are able to be present in each infinitely small moment, when we are aware of the relationship with all things rather than just the time on the clock—then we start to be able to listen and respond with *"Hineni."*

If we take the time to step into timelessness whenever we are faced with fears of the future, we can find, like Daniel, that the complicated turns of life are easier to understand. We can guide ourselves and others as a result of our being present in the moment. When we truly pause and listen, we can understand things that confused us before, and let go of our fears of the future as we deepen our relationship with the Divine. As Rabbi Steve Robbins is fond of saying, "God doesn't shout, God whispers." Hear the whisper of the Divine in each moment, and then, like Daniel shows, all moments become clearer. The conscious use of ritual and preparation allows each of us to recognize the deep truth found in this book: all of our judgments are, in fact, God's.

Breathe. Let go. Be present. Listen. As we each hear the Divine whisper in each moment, all moments become filled with clarity, wholeness, and peace.

Notes

1. The book of Daniel is not in the Prophets (Neviʾim) section of the Bible but rather in the Writings (Ketuvim).

2. While not in the traditional format and practices, this has some of the spirit of the ancient practices.

3. Yogi Bhajan, *The Aquarian Teacher* (Espanola, NM: Kundalini Research Institute, 1969), 129.

9

Esther: Even Where God Isn't . . . God Is

All the Festivals will be annulled in future time, except for
Purim.

—*Midrash Mishlei* 9:2

The book of Esther is one of the five scrolls of Ketuvim that are
associated with a holiday, in this case, Purim. This holiday is celebrated every year in late winter or early spring, and its practices
include giving gifts to the poor, dressing up, and getting so drunk
that you cannot tell between good and evil. It also includes listening to the recitation of the book of Esther, and hearing this tale
that is so argued about by everyone from ancient sages to modern
commentators.

Set in the fifth century BCE, the book of Esther takes place entirely in the Diaspora, the Jewish communities outside of Israel.
In this case, the setting is Persia during the kingship of Ahasuerus
(usually identified as either Xerxes I or Artaxerxes II), in the city
of Shushan. Ahasuerus is married to Queen Vashti, and has many
ministers, one of whom is Haman. The king has a large banquet
and tells his eunuchs to bring Vashti "before the king wearing a
royal diadem, to display her beauty to the peoples and the

officials" (1:11, JPS); Vashti refuses. For this refusal, Vashti is stripped of her crown and banished from the kingdom. The king then appoints officers to find beautiful young women for him who will be bathed and prepared, and one of whom will become the new queen.

A Jew named Mordecai is the foster father to a young woman, Esther (it is unclear whether he is an uncle or cousin, or what the exact blood relationship is, but he had adopted her as his daughter when her parents died). When Esther is taken to be prepared with the other women, Mordecai suggests that she keep her identity as a Jew a secret, and she is treated with great respect by the other servants of the harem. After a year of preparation, when Esther is taken to the king, she finds favor with him and he makes her queen. Early in her position as queen, Mordecai hears some guards talking about assassinating the king, tells Esther, who tells the king, saving his life and being entered into the royal annals.

Haman, as the king's chief minister, parades around town having people bow to him; he has incredible hatred for Mordecai the Jew, who will not bow down. (Some commentaries say this is because Mordecai would not bow to the images of idols on the robe of Haman.) Haman plots to kill all Jews, and convinces the king to let Haman have all the Jews in his kingdom killed. When Mordecai finds out about this, he is devastated, and prays fervently for a miracle. Mordecai asks for Esther to help by appealing to the king, but she refuses on the basis that anyone going to see the king without being summoned could be executed. Only after Mordecai reminds her that God will save the Jews and she may not be saved if she does not help does she agree to go before Ahasuerus. The Jews of Shushan fast for three days, praying for her to be helped, and she goes to visit the king:

> On the third day, Esther put on royal apparel and stood in the inner court of the king's palace, facing the king's palace, while the king was sitting on his royal throne in the throne room facing the entrance of the palace. As soon as the king saw Queen Esther standing in the court, she won his favor.

> The king extended to Esther the golden scepter which he had
> in his hand, and Esther approached and touched the tip of
> the scepter. "What troubles you, Queen Esther?" the king
> asked her. "And what is your request? Even to half the king-
> dom, it shall be granted you." (5:1-3, JPS)

Esther asks the king to bring Haman and join her at a feast. At the
feast, she asks that they return the next day for another feast that
she would prepare. Haman brags about his success to his wife, as
well as his anger at Mordecai the Jew, who still refuses to bow
down. His wife suggests putting up a large pole to impale
Mordecai, and then having the king decree to do that the next day.
Haman prepares the pole and looks forward to getting the king's
approval to impale Mordecai.

That night, Ahasuerus has trouble sleeping, and has the annals
of his kingship read to him. When he hears of Mordecai's earlier
report of the assassins, he summons Haman and asks Haman what
should be done for someone whom the king wants to honor.
Haman, thinking that the king is referring to him, suggests that
the king should honor a person by putting him on a royal horse
in royal garb accompanied by a noble crying out how great the
man is. Much to Haman's disappointment and humiliation, the
king tells Haman to do just that with Mordecai the Jew.

At the second feast with the king and Haman that night, Esther
makes her request for her people, and names Haman as their
enemy. The enraged king leaves the banquet room, and Haman
begs Esther for his life. When the king storms back in, he sees
Haman "lying prostrate on the couch on which Esther reclined.
'Does he mean,' cried the king, 'to ravage the queen in my own
palace?' No sooner did these words leave the king's lips than
Haman's face was covered" (7:8, JPS). The king then has Haman
impaled on the stake originally set up for Mordecai. Haman's
property is given to Esther, and Mordecai becomes a minister for
the king. Ahasuerus tells Mordecai to write whatever edict he
would like concerning the Jews, and he will enforce it with his
royal signet. Mordecai gives permission for all Jews to "destroy,

massacre, and exterminate" (8:11, JPS) anyone who seeks to hurt them.

On the thirteenth day of the month of Adar, the Jews killed their enemies. Haman's ten sons were killed, as well as seventy-five thousand enemies (9:16), and the Jews then celebrated on the fourteenth and fifteenth of Adar with a feast and merrymaking. Because Haman had originally decided upon the date of killing the Jews by drawing a lot (a lottery ticket, *pur* in Hebrew, the plural is *purim*), Mordecai and Esther obligated all Jews to celebrate the holiday of "Purim" to commemorate the victory. The book ends describing the holiday that is still celebrated today as the Bible commands it by Jews around the world.

This is the story that is read every year, the basics of which are known by Jewish children around the world. Esther becomes queen to Ahasuerus; Haman tries to kill the people; Mordecai and Esther save the people; and we commemorate the holiday annually. On Purim people dress up in costumes, play games, and drink (adults only). Many synagogues throughout the world have Purim carnivals to celebrate the happy events.

A Present God in the Midst of Absence?

But are these events really so happy? Is it righteous to celebrate what is ultimately a military victory that led to the deaths of seventy-five thousand people? (Many synagogues leave out the paragraph about the massacre from their public reading of the book of Esther on Purim so as not to bring up this challenging issue.) Out of all the holy holidays and festivals in the calendar, this is the one that will be celebrated in future times, when all others are not? Maybe there is another teaching to be found here that is more relevant than an ancient military victory.

There are many discussions in the Talmud, as well as with later commentators, about some of the problems inherent in the book of Esther, but there is one problem that eclipses all others: this is the only book of the Bible in which God is never mentioned. Nowhere is God's name present in this book. God is seemingly absent.

This may be the opening for a deep teaching from this ancient text that is useful in our lives today, and an answer to some of the persistent questions in this world of chaos: Where is God when God is apparently not around? What drives God to hide himself? What can we do to discover God in those times?

We live in a culture and time of excess. Information and entertainment are readily and quickly available, as are sex, drugs, and alcohol. There are more examples of the norm of excessive behavior now than there has been at any time in history. Universities around the country have sponsored "foam parties," where college students come to a football field that has been covered with four or more feet of bubbles and dance. Usually drunk before they even get there, students come in bathing suits, and you never know what really happens under the foam. Underwear and bathing suits are found left on the field, students talk about never knowing who really was touching them where, and hospitalizations for rape abound after these events. Las Vegas, the largest tourist city in the nation, continues its ad campaign of "What happens in Vegas, stays in Vegas." Hundreds of thousands of people use their presence in Las Vegas at a convention, in New Orleans during Mardi Gras, or in Fort Lauderdale during spring break as an excuse to act out and be excessive. They get caught up in the fun, alcohol, and sexuality; and women who are normally shy find themselves drunk and showing their breasts in exchange for a twenty-five-cent necklace of plastic beads. Alcoholism is one of the fastest growing problems on college campuses in the country, as are dramatic increases in alcohol poisoning. It isn't just a social problem, though, as we find the need for excess inherently underlying the actions of so many political leaders who may not be drunk with alcohol but are drunk with power and, like addicts, are constantly searching for more. Where is God in all of this? Where is God in the midst of drunken debauchery, political arrogance, and sexual overindulgences? The book of Esther shows us not only an answer to that question but also provides us with a pathway to get out of the chaos that inevitably ensues after excess.

Excess, Addictions, and Role Models

There is another way of looking at Esther besides the perspective of Mordecai and Esther being heroes and leading the Jews to a victory. It is more painful to explore, but for all of us who live in a time of excess, it may be significantly more useful.

Let's look at what ties together all the characters of this play, so written like a classic Greek piece of theater. Ahasuerus likes to have parties and drink . . . a lot. His name can even be translated as "a pain in the head," as in a constant state of drunkenness or hangover. His excess is an addiction to alcohol, and leads not only to a sexual addiction (with his harem) but also to letting others rule his kingdom on his behalf. In his drunken state he even loses his queen Vashti, when he asks her to dance for his ministers. Interestingly, the text is clear about what she will be wearing: a royal diadem. No wonder she doesn't want to show up to his party. Dancing with just a royal crown on in front of your king's buddies (who are all drunk) doesn't sound like a particularly fun (or safe) night.

Haman too is drunk. He is drunk with power. Each time he gets the smallest increase in his political power, he schemes and plots for more. When Mordecai is the one person who doesn't bow to him, he needs to have the entire Jewish population killed. When Mordecai irritates him again, he raises up a pole to impale him. He is a "drunk" as well, only with his need to acquire power instead of alcohol.

Even our heroine is excessive and a "drunk" in her relationship with her own sexuality and beauty. She becomes queen at the suggestion of Mordecai, and is happy to be pampered with baths and cosmetics. But it is only when she is threatened that she consents to approach the king. Like any addict, she is concerned at first primarily with her own well-being. Even when she goes to approach the king, she relies upon her sexuality:

> The king extended to Esther the golden scepter which he had in his hand, and Esther approached and touched the tip of the scepter. "What troubles you, Queen Esther?" the king asked her. "And what is your request? Even to half the kingdom, it shall be granted you." (5:2-3, JPS)

Given that the Bible is filled with double entendres, does it really make any sense that this drunken king is holding a physical scepter in his hand, and that by her touching the tip of the scepter he is willing to give her anything, even up to half the kingdom? Or is the text implying that while he might call what he was holding in his hand a "scepter" as a euphemism, it might in actuality be a physical part of him rather than a jeweled object of royalty? And if this drunken king is in fact holding a part of his anatomy in his hand, suddenly it becomes a lot easier to believe that he would give half his kingdom to Esther because of the way she touches the tip of it. Looking at the text from that perspective, Esther clearly has no issue about using her beauty for her own goals. Later, during the feast when Ahasuerus storms out in anger at Haman, he comes back to see Haman "lying prostrate on the couch." Is it so hard to believe that Esther wants him there, specifically so that Haman will be executed upon the return of the king? From this perspective of the text, it would seem that Esther is a beautiful woman who is "drunk" on her own beauty and sexuality—how to use it and what she can achieve through it.

Through this lens, even the great hero Mordecai gets caught in the world of excess, ultimately becoming drunk on power. He is an honorable and good man throughout the majority of the text. He takes in Esther when she is orphaned, and keeps true to his values when Haman wants him to bow. He prays devoutly and has faith that the Jews will be redeemed with or without Esther's

help. But when he is put in power after Haman's demise, he becomes the personification of the saying "Power tends to corrupt,
and absolute power corrupts absolutely."[1] He uses his new power
to massacre seventy-five thousand people. Rather than making
them his friends, or even servants, he chooses to destroy their lives
entirely. Once he has the taste of power (in the drunken king's
name), he abuses it, again getting caught in the drunkenness of
excess.

Looking at the book of Esther this way, we see a common thread
tying together the main characters: they are all drunk and excessive in one way or another. Ahasuerus is drunk on alcohol, Esther
on her beauty, and Mordecai and Haman on power. The entire
story is excessive and over the top, and filled with negative role
models.[2]

It's a difficult implication: that the book of Esther is filled with
negative role models of how not to act. That part of its purpose is
to show us the effect of drunkenness in a multiplicity of forms.
But that also makes the rabbinic commandment that we should
get so drunk on Purim that we "cannot tell the difference between
'cursed be Haman' and 'blessed be Mordecai'" (Talmud, *Megillah*
7b, Soncino). It is in this practice that goes back to the Talmud that
we can find some clearer gleanings of what the book of Esther has
to teach us.

Each year, we are commanded to get so drunk that we cannot
tell the difference between blessing the "hero" of this book and
cursing the "villain." On a simplistic level, there is a correlation
between the two as the numerical value of each phrase is the same.
(In gematria, both "cursed is Haman" and "blessed is Mordecai"
equal 502 in Hebrew.) But on a more practical level, it seems as if
the sages are leading us to be clear that there is little difference
between the men in certain ways. Both are drunk on power. Both
try to arrange to have people massacred, and Mordecai is successful in his endeavor. It is one of the most valuable of lessons: anyone
can become excessive, addicted to one's behavior, and drunk on
excess.

Embracing the Shadow, Unifying with the Light, and Being Willing to Walk Away

For one night a year, Jews around the world embrace this practice. For one night a year, God is apparently hidden as we get so drunk that we cannot tell between the two characters. We embrace the excess consciously for one night. In some ways, it is a very Jungian concept: to embrace the shadow consciously one night per year so that it doesn't control us the rest of the year. Through the process of drinking and hearing the tale of Esther, we embrace the darkness consciously and then release it fully so that it has no hold on us.

Although God is never specifically mentioned in this book of excess, the Divine Presence can be felt throughout it. As Mordecai reminds Esther, she may have been placed in that very position of power in order to save the Jews. Even in the chaos of excess and drunkenness, God is present, subtly guiding us to where we need to be. It is our choice what to do, and whether we will choose to act with integrity or lose ourselves in the process. But God is always present in the midst of the craziness of anything, even a foam party.

There is another model that we can learn from in this interpretation of the text as well. The ancient rabbis of the Talmud were hard on Vashti, calling her wicked and vain among other things. But the text as written gives us a different model of behavior: a model of strength. Vashti says no to the tyrant through her refusal to dance for the king's ministers. In the midst of a game of excess, she refuses to play. (This is one of the reasons that Vashti became a heroine to the feminist movement, being notably glorified by Harriet Beecher Stowe among others.) In the middle of excess, she walks away. This too is a model of behavior that we can use in today's world.

When confronted with the push to be excessive, Vashti teaches us that the wise thing to do is to walk away from the circumstance. Although we can stay in the midst of the chaos for a while and retain our senses, the lesson of Mordecai is that anyone can fall into the trap of getting "drunk" on something and lose control of one's behavior. Vashti's actions are an illustration of what we can do when confronted with a chaos that we know can overwhelm us: walk away. Leave. If everyone else is getting drunk and dancing at a party in Vegas, and you don't want to get caught up in it (and do something that you may regret the next day, or decade), then take the lesson of Vashti. She walked away from her throne rather than succumb to the craziness that she knew would happen if she played the game that the king wanted.

This is a teaching that is repeated in many forms throughout Jewish history. Our sages often teach that we are not to get too close to certain practices, as they will lead us away from our soul's purpose. If the business practices around us are unethical, we need to have the faith that God will help us work things out as we leave the environment. If relationships are toxic because of addictive behavior, we need to have the courage and willingness to walk away in order to stay true to who we are. Vashti teaches us to not get caught up in the game and to remember what is really important. We need to be constantly aware, especially when surrounded by excess, that (to paraphrase the nineteenth-century philosopher and priest Teilhard de Chardin) we are spiritual beings having a human experience, and not human beings that are occasionally spiritual. While there is much good that can be accomplished if we can keep our senses while the situation and people around us are getting "drunk," we must also be self-aware enough to know that it is extremely difficult to not get caught up in the chaos. We must be willing to walk away before we become like Mordecai and get so caught up in the excess that there becomes little difference between us and Haman. Even in future times, it may be that we can get excessive and become drunk in one way or another, and perhaps this is why the holiday of Purim is said to be the one holiday that will still be observed. The book of Esther teaches us to be careful of that chaos.

The book of Esther teaches us to beware of excess, to experience it consciously once a year so that it doesn't overwhelm us, and to walk away from it rather than lose ourselves and become drunk in one way or another. But there is also the teaching that God moves quietly yet clearly in the midst of chaos. It is a good thing to remember that according to the book of Genesis, before the earth was created, there was only *tohu v'vohu*, "chaos and confusion" (see Gen 1:2). Countless artists and musicians create as a result of the chaos in their lives, sometimes caused by addictions, and more often caused by the circumstances of chaos that created the addictions. This too may be a reason that the sages of old insisted that we consciously dive into the chaos of excess once a year: so that we feel the power and the danger of *tohu v'vohu*. By stepping into it consciously, we have a clearer opportunity to see God's hand everywhere, even in the craziness.

Look at the models found in this book, and use them. When those around you seem crazy with excessive desires, make the conscious decision of how far you are willing to go with them. Be clear that anyone has the potential to lose oneself in the drunkenness of a group experience. Be aware of your own limits and be constantly vigilant about your own behavior. Always be willing to emulate Vashti and just walk away. It may seem difficult at first, but leaving the dangerous situation is often the best thing you can do for yourself and others.

As a rabbi who leads Purim services, I have found another personal lesson, but it is difficult to choreograph. When people are drunk in whatever way, whether it's alcohol, a psychotropic substance, or anything else, they are often more open psychospiritually than they are when sober. Their defenses are often down, and if I have a clear intention, I have found that it is possible to have meaningful conversations with people who are drunk such that their behavior dramatically shifts in the future. People are often receptive when they are in the midst of their excess to concepts (especially spiritual concepts) that they would reject when their minds are more in control. But my experience is that it is important that if you wish to experience God in this type of dialogue, then it has to be timed just at the point in their excess where they have let go of their psychological armor, but not so far as their being totally out of control in the chaos. Again, it is a fine line between Mordecai as the hero of his people and Mordecai getting lost in power and killing tens of thousands.

Read the book of Esther whenever you need a reminder of how people can lose control. It is a short book, and written like a piece of theater. Use it as a reminder to not let yourself get caught up in the group behavior of others that is excessive and can lead you to losing yourself, your purpose, and your essence. Realize that drunkenness can include many other things besides alcohol, and take responsibility for your own actions.

Most importantly, when you are caught in an environment that has lost itself in the chaos of excess, listen carefully for the voice of God whispering to you. Use the chaos as an opportunity to be in a relationship with the Divine. Let the confusion become a backdrop on which you can create through your listening to the quietness that is inside. Make the conscious decision to transform the profane into the sacred, and to be the instrument of sanity in the chaos. The sages teach that in the same way that Esther is hidden in the palace (the court doesn't see her as the Jew that she is), God is often hidden in the world. Look for Her.

There is a story told by many clergy of different faiths about a grandfather whose little granddaughter came to him, crying. "Why are you crying?" he asked. She replied, "We were all playing hide-and-seek. It was my turn to hide, and no one came to look for me." With a tear in his eye, her loving grandfather said, "Now you know how God feels."

Let the story of Esther remind you how to look for God in the chaos without being confused, and how to respond to the excesses of the modern world in ways that bring light, harmony, and peace.[3]

Notes

1. John Emerich Edward Dalberg Acton, 1st Baron Acton (Letter, 1887).

2. As discussed in the introduction, this perspective, although important and valid as an interpretation, is not the most common interpretation
of the text as a piece on the virtues of faith, courage, and redemption.
Additionally, it is not meant to invalidate the normative interpretation,
but to add other levels of additional understanding that can be used in
modern society.

3. For further (and more common) understandings about the book of
Esther, the reader is encouraged to study any of the wonderful commentaries both ancient and modern that reflect the powerful lessons
found in the courage of Esther, the faith of Mordecai, and the interpretations of God's face being hidden.

10

Ezra-Nehemiah-Chronicles: Spirit Becomes Substance

And it shall come to pass in the end of days that the mountain of the House of God will be established at the top of the mountains and will be exalted above the hills, and all nations will flow to it.

—Isaiah 2:2 (ArtScroll)

There is a Native American saying among many tribes that teaches that all the spirituality in the world doesn't mean anything if it doesn't grow corn to feed the children. As each of the books of Ketuvim have been explored, we have found that the sages of old have taught, through these books, how to have a clearer and more intimate experience with God in nearly every type of relationship. Each book has guided us into a way of knowing more, appreciating more, and experiencing more of the Divine in each moment. But how does that affect us, and once we can have that type of awareness, what do we do with it?

The books of Ezra, Nehemiah, and Chronicles are the answers. These are the books of Ketuvim that teach us what can be done once we are willing to see and accept God as an integral part of every experience and relationship we have in life. These are the manuals that collectively demonstrate what can and needs to be done when we start to have more awareness of the beauty, compassion, and presence of God in every place, at every time, in every way. Because they do this collectively, these books are combined in this final discussion about the books of Ketuvim.

Before going into the content and teachings of these books themselves, it is important to recognize the theology behind the temple, its destruction, its rebuilding, and ultimately the promise of what the temple means, as this is such an important topic, especially for Ezra-Nehemiah.

The World Is the Temple

While there is a disagreement regarding specific dates between secular academics and traditional rabbinic sources (primarily *Seder Olam Rabbah* from the second century CE), the importance and progression of the creation, destruction, rebuilding, destruction, and promise of a temple rebuilt again is a journey that must be briefly discussed before understanding these books. As discussed earlier, King Solomon built the temple in Jerusalem after the death of his father, King David. It was the highlight of his reign, and became the symbol (or location, depending on your belief) of God's presence in the physical world. The temple housed the sacred objects from the journey through the desert, such as the holy ark, and was the central point in the religious worship of the Jews. It was more than a building, but an entire complex dedicated to God and to the physical manifestation of God in the world. It was considered to be the footstool of the Almighty here on earth.

When the temple was destroyed by King Nebuchadnezzar in 586 BCE,[1] the holy items were taken and dispersed. Some were taken to Babylon and lost as that empire was conquered by other nations, some were hidden away by Jews, and some few remained in Jerusalem. As we learned in the book of Daniel, the Jews were spread throughout the world, without a national homeland or a central place of worship. But each day the Jews were away from the temple, they prayed that it would be rebuilt in their time. Ultimately, it was rebuilt under the guidance of Ezra and Nehemiah, but was again destroyed centuries later by the Romans in 70 CE. The promises of a future third temple have been kept alive as one of the primary prayers and anchors of the Jewish people for the last two thousand years, as its rebuilding is considered to be a sign of the Messiah's coming and a time of peace in the world.

One of the simplest ways of phrasing the importance of it is to quote Napoleon, who wondered what the Jews in Paris were doing when on Tisha B'Av, the holiday observing the destruction of the temple, he heard wailing from the synagogue. When told that they were all mourning the destruction of the temple, he is said to have exclaimed, "If the Jews are still crying after 1,800 years, then I am certain the temple will be rebuilt." Even the great conqueror of Europe understood that a culture willing to wait for that long with the same hope is so deeply committed to the idea that the hope will someday become a reality.

When the first temple was destroyed, it was the most painful experience as a culture that the Jews could imagine. The words of Lamentations that we have studied are expressions of the horrors and depression that came about with that destruction. The only hope that the Jews of that time had was that someday the temple would be rebuilt. This was the environment that both Ezra and Nehemiah experienced, and the situation that each of them would resolve to change.

Originally, the books of Ezra and Nehemiah were combined into one text under Ezra. Although it was recognized early on that much of that text was written by Nehemiah, it was not until centuries later that the text was split into the two books that we find today in our Bibles (there are some very traditional Hebraic Bibles that still keep them as one book). The stories of these men and the lessons of their lives are philosophically combined and, along with Chronicles, guide us into what can and must be done when we start to experience God in every relationship in our lives.

Ezra the Lawgiver

Ezra lived in Babylon in the time after the destruction of the first temple, and was a descendant of the high priest. He was the disciple and student of Baruch ben Neriah, who in turn was the scribe of the prophet Jeremiah. King Cyrus of Persia had become king, conquering the Babylonian Empire, and was significantly friendlier to the Jewish exiles from Judah than the Babylonian rulers had been. A priest and spiritual leader, the Talmud teaches, "Ezra was worthy for the Torah to have been given to Israel through him, had Moses not preceded him" (*Sanhedrin* 21b, Schottenstein); and he is often known as "Ezra the Lawgiver." A scribe, scholar, and leader of the people, Ezra was given permission by Cyrus to lead the Hebrews back into Jerusalem and to reestablish the spiritual teachings there. Ezra did not go with the first wave of Jews back to Jerusalem; his teacher, Baruch, was too old to travel and Ezra would not leave his teacher. After the death of Baruch ben Neriah, Ezra traveled to Jerusalem and began to rebuild the moral fiber and enforce the spiritual laws of the people. He became the flame that burned and lit up the physical temple that was being built through his spiritual guidance.

Ezra is also considered to be the founder of the Great Assembly, which later became the Sanhedrin. A collection of the greatest Jewish minds and hearts of the period, they became the interpreters and messengers of the Oral Law. Without the tools of the first temple—specifically the high priest's breastplate, which was also a "magical" object that could make judgments and prophesy but had been lost in the destruction—it became important to congregate a group of knowledgeable elders who would be able to serve as judges based on the laws of the Torah. If Ezra was the flame that lit the second temple, this group, led by him, became the full lighting system.

Ezra, who was not only educated but also wise, created the spiritual nation of Israel. He helped the people recognize God in their hearts, and guided them to embrace that Divinity through their practices of the commandments of Torah. He created a community that looked at all the world as a physical expression of Divine spirituality, and reignited the spiritual light of the people who had been in exile.

Nehemiah: Building the Holy

Nehemiah was the partner and balance to Ezra. Where Ezra developed the spiritual boundaries, skills, and practices, Nehemiah was concerned with the building of walls, gates, and laws that would allow the culture to survive. Together, they blended their talents and insights into rebuilding both the temple and the city of Jerusalem.

Nehemiah was a servant to the Persian king, and was deeply disturbed that more of his Jewish brothers and sisters did not take up the king's offer to repopulate Jerusalem (only 42,360 people went back to Israel, according to Ezra 2:64). His pain over the special place "where my forefathers are buried" (Neh 2:3, ArtScroll) led him to beseech the king to let him rebuild the city. The king made him governor of Judah and sent him to fortify and rebuild the city of Jerusalem. He rebuilt the walls and gates of the city, and was an honest leader after a series of corrupt governors before him. Together with Ezra as the spiritual leader, who was already in Jerusalem, Nehemiah started to enforce laws that prohibited violating the Sabbath and other Jewish commandments. After twelve years of helping to put together the internal structure of the new society in Jerusalem, he returned to Persia, but came back to Jerusalem years later to find that the society was once again having community challenges. He cleansed the temple, and the book of Nehemiah ends with him recapitulating his accomplishments and asking God to remember him for good.

Nehemiah's personality can be most clearly seen when he asked the king to go to Jerusalem:

> The king said to me, "What is your request?" I then prayed
> to the God of heaven. And I said to the king, "If it pleases the

king, and if your servant finds favor before you, then permit
me to go to Judah to the city where my ancestors are buried,
so that I may build it." (Neh 2:4-5, ArtScroll)

Looking more deeply at this one passage, we can learn a great
deal not only about Nehemiah but also about how we can begin
to use the many lessons that we have discovered in this biblical
section of Ketuvim.

At first glance, it seems as if Nehemiah was appealing to the
king of Persia, and made his prayer to God (which is not explicitly
detailed) as an afterthought. But the reality is much deeper, subtle,
and more important than that.

Nehemiah's prayer is not listed in the text because the words
themselves were the prayer. Multiple commentators point out that
while he was speaking to the king of Persia, he was really address-
ing the heavenly King. For Nehemiah, who saw Divinity in all
aspects of life and in every relationship, each dialogue that he was
involved with had at its heart a dialogue with God. His love of
God was so ingrained and deep within him, that even the words
said to a foreign king were in actuality a prayer to the Almighty.
This is an example of the greatness of Nehemiah. He was able to
take the most mundane tasks, and always see God within them.
He wasn't needed to help make the temple itself holy (which had
been built more than a decade before he came to Jerusalem), but
he transformed every action of building the city, supporting it into
a holy action through his constant and consistent intention. While
Ezra built the spiritual fire with holiness, Nehemiah built the
physical protection for it. Ezra's actions were clearly spiritual,
while Nehemiah's were more hidden in the process of physically
creating and supporting the spiritual relationship of the people
with God.

If Ezra reignited the spark of holy light within Jerusalem on a
spiritual level, Nehemiah can be considered to be the architect of
consciously creating the structure around that light. Nowhere is
this more evident than in chapter 8 of the book of Nehemiah. Ezra
was called to read the Torah publicly for the people, who had not

heard the words for many years. There, he read from the twenty-third chapter of the book of Vayikra (Leviticus), where the people were commanded to dwell in sukkot (booths) for a week. This commandment, still practiced today, involves each family building a temporary structure and dwelling in it for the duration of the holiday of Sukkot. It is a reminder of the temporal quality of the physical world, and of the need to consciously rely on God for our needs. This holiday is associated with the patriarch Jacob (Jacob died on the first night of the festival, and the word *Sukkot* is actually first found in reference to him in the Torah—Gen 33:17); and Jacob is also the patriarch associated with the temple itself. (He is commonly associated in the Hasidic and Kabbalistic teachings as being tied to praying with God in a structure, as opposed to Isaac, who prays in a field, and Abraham, who prays on the mountain.) The first festival that Nehemiah and Ezra reinstate is the practice of building a holy structure.

The sukkah is also a beautiful metaphor for Nehemiah and Ezra. The sukkah is where people sleep, eat, pray, and dwell in all ways, but it has one thing that is clearly absent from any temple: an Eternal Light (symbolizing the constant presence of God among other things). The sukkah is the holy structure, in the same way that Nehemiah is a holy architect. The light is brought through the words of Torah and the work of Ezra. Together, they are able to bring the Holy into the world.

This is the brilliance of Nehemiah. He made holy structures, containers that would be able to hold the Divine Spirit in subtle ways. He had such love for God that each conversation (with a king or a worker), each action, was motivated underneath by his constant experience of the Divine in everything. The sages teach that because of that all-pervading love, he was the perfect instrument to rebuild the city itself.

The Anchor of the Sabbath

But rebuilding the city and the temple weren't enough, as we see later in this book. When Nehemiah returned to Jerusalem after being gone, he found that the people were once again acting inappropriately: they had lost an awareness of their personal and collective relationships with the Divine. So Nehemiah gave the great solution, the great remedy, for people who continue to forget their relationship with God: he enforced the observance of the Sabbath (Neh 13:19). He prohibited trading and commerce, and reinstituted the practice of dedicating that day fully to God—one day out of the workplace and spent with consciousness about the Divine. It's a rich practice that has been all too often forgotten about in the busyness of the twenty-first century, but Nehemiah shows us how important it is as a reminder to ourselves about our personal experience of Divinity at least once a week.

In enforcing the laws of the Sabbath, Nehemiah gives a teaching that could only come from a man of commerce, physicality, and politics. When clergy or prophets demand that the Sabbath be observed, many people think that this is an easy thing for the clergy because they don't have to work for a living in the same way. But when a man of commerce and action like Nehemiah demonstrates how important the Sabbath is, it gains credibility in the eyes of the masses. This is the other great teaching of the book of Nehemiah: when we are starting to be unaware of our experience of God in any circumstance, it is important to go back to the root practice. Celebrate the Sabbath. Take one day off and dedicate it to nonphysical issues. If Nehemiah could do it, we all can.

This is an incredibly deep teaching when integrated with the entire philosophy of this book. If we can truly begin to experience God in every type of relationship, as we have learned from Ketuvim, we need to have an "anchor" practice to help us remember our priorities when they get lost in the hustle and bustle of the working world. This anchor is the Sabbath. Nehemiah teaches us that if we "let go and let God" for one day, it affects the other six significantly. If we fully celebrate the Sabbath, then the rest of the week becomes a time when we can find it easier to experience the Divinity in every moment, experience, and relationship. Together Ezra, Nehemiah, and the Sabbath become the guides to reinstate the sanctity, not only of the temple, but also of the land itself.

Chronicles:
Where Have We Been, and Where Are We Going?

Let's turn for a moment to the other book in this section of
Ketuvim, the book of Chronicles. This text is an unembellished
account of history from the birth of Adam through the invitation
of Cyrus, the king of Persia, to rebuild the temple:

> Thus said Cyrus, King of Persia, All the kingdoms of the Earth
> has the Lord God of heaven given me; and he has charged
> me to build him a house in Jerusalem, which is in Judah.
> Whoever is among you of all his people, the Lord his God be
> with him, and let him go up. (2 Chr 36:23, ArtScroll)

The vast majority of Chronicles recapitulates what has been written earlier in the Tanakh, mostly from the books of Samuel and
Kings. Although originally one text, it is usually split into the two
books titled 1 Chronicles and 2 Chronicles. The first third of
1 Chronicles is a straight list of genealogy from Adam to King
David, and the last two-thirds of that section are more detailed
accounts from David's life. Second Chronicles then spends a third
of its writing on the details of King Solomon's life, and the last
two-thirds recount incidents that lead up to and end with Cyrus's
invitation to rebuild the house of God. The entire text reads like
(and, according to many academics, actually is) the records from
a king's library, much like the congressional record of today details
the actions of the congress. The Tanakh begins in Genesis with the
creation of the Universe, and ends with Chronicles: specifically
ending with the promise of a rebuilt temple.

Given that the books of Ezra and Nehemiah take place after
Cyrus's invitation, it would seem that the canonical order should
be Ezra after Chronicles, which is a hint that there is a deeper
meaning here. The entire Bible ends with the promise of the temple
as a conscious statement by the sages of old. It is an implication
that all of creation leads up to the rebuilding of the temple. The
zenith of the journey to that goal is found in the lives of King
David and his son, King Solomon, but the real key is that Chroni-

cles is making it clear that the purpose of creation becomes manifest in the creation of a house of God that will have "all nations flow to it" (Isa 2:2, ArtScroll). The invitation at the end of Chronicles is not said by a king or priest of Israel, but by a foreign king. The promise of the temple is for all nations, all of whom will come to the sacred mountain in Jerusalem. If we remember that traditionally the temple was considered a physical manifestation of God's presence on earth, then the purpose of Chronicles becomes clear: that Presence will manifest itself for everyone.

There is a wonderful technique for teaching meditation that involves an orange. Students hold their own orange, studying it visually, smelling it, really looking deeply at it. They see it in their mind's eye, and as they open and eventually eat the orange, they keep repeating the process inside their own mind. As they are doing this, they remain conscious of the fact that their orange was created specifically for them. All the orange trees before the one that gave birth to their orange, all the roots, leaves, and branches of their tree, have come to fruition in the singular piece of fruit that they are holding. On a certain level, all the history of oranges have culminated in that one moment of the orange that is in their hand. Its entire purpose of existence will be fulfilled with their eating of it. Students often respond that the sense of gratitude they feel for an orange changes their entire outlook on life. Chronicles is a written version of that orange meditation: all of creation culminates with the rebuilding of the sacred and Divine in the physical world.

Integrating that purpose of Chronicles along with the tales and teachings of Ezra and Nehemiah is a perfect way to understand why these are the ending texts to this beautiful section of Ketuvim. Each of the books of Ketuvim, from Ruth through Esther, guides the reader to have a clear and personal experience of God in every relationship of Life. Whatever the experience in our physical lives, these books help us experience Divinity in each moment with each person and encounter that we have. Ezra-Nehemiah-Chronicles teaches us what to do with that knowledge: build. Build a life on earth that helps all people experience the Divine in every moment (as the ancient temple did for those who came to it). Build a structure composed of both the material and the physical. Build a container and light the spark of Divinity in it. But these books do more than just enjoin us in what we need to do; they give us the process to achieve success in doing it.

If we realize that every moment really is a Divine gift, every breath a demonstration of God in our lives, then the only response that we can have is one of gratitude. That gratitude combines with a desire to help others also have the same ecstatic experience. Ezra-Nehemiah-Chronicles shows us how to express that gratitude as an integration of what we have hopefully learned and experienced through the other books of Ketuvim. Like Ezra, we need to accept the blessings of the moment, and be committed to helping others have their own experience. Like Nehemiah, we need to make every moment of our lives sacred and make everything we do a holy act. We need to remember that we are only men and women, and that we can easily forget "sacredness" in the chaos of the world events. But Nehemiah also teaches us to anchor ourselves with a personal practice of taking one day per week and dedicating it to our spiritual renewal. As we make the conscious choice of experiencing God in every moment, then we recognize that each moment is the flower of a Tree of Life that extends back all the way to the beginning of time.

All the "spiritual" awareness means nothing if it "doesn't grow corn to feed the children." Ezra, Nehemiah, and Chronicles are the manuals to teach us how to take what we have learned in the other books of Ketuvim and manifest our experience into everyday life. These are the books that guide us to not only know the Sacred but also to make every moment holy in the world.

Note

1. There is a dialogue about the year, with some tracking the date to 422 BCE, although 586 BCE is the most commonly accepted date.

Conclusion: The Journey in Every Place

Why is God called Makom *("place")? Because in every place where the righteous stand, God stands with them, as it is written, "In every place (makom) where I cause My name to be mentioned, I will come to you and bless you" (Exod 20:21). And it is written: "Jacob reached the makom, and H/he lodged there" (Gen 28:11).*

—*Pirkei de-Rabbi Eliezer*, first/second-century commentary

This quote from the Talmudic sage Rabbi Eliezer—the disciple of the great Rabbi Yochanan ben Zakkai and the teacher of Rabbi Akiva—expresses a wonderful understanding of the concepts of experiencing God in every place and recognizing that every experience is embedded with the Divine Presence. Rabbi Eliezer, who led both a glorious and tortured life, understood experiencing God in every place. First disowned and then ultimately supremely honored by his father for his scholarship, Rabbi Eliezer was both a leader of the Talmudic dialogues and at one point excommunicated from the Great Assembly. He died with the greatest of honors by his students and all the community of Israel. He was the student and teacher of some of the greatest mystics and legal experts of the Talmud, and he lived a life with every possible emotion included in it. Through it all, he was able to see and experience God in every place, in every moment.

This is the gift of Ketuvim. If we embrace each book fully and use each of them as a manual to experience God in multiple types of relationships, we can learn to be aware of God in every place and every time. The awareness of the Divine becomes the foundation and fabric of every experience we have. The result is a level of depth and joy that creates a sense of gratitude, and that—as was discussed in the previous chapter—guides us into making everything around us more holy and sacred.

The original order of the books of Ketuvim, in *Bava Batra*, is also a deep lesson in the psycho-emotional growth of a human being; perhaps that is part of the reason why the books were originally structured in that order. Although placed in the order of a human being's growth, they are all meant to be interpreted as adults on a spiritual journey, which is parallel to the earlier psychological journey from childhood into and through maturity that we each experience as we grow up.

When a child is born, it is very difficult for her to intellectually understand any concept of "God." The child relates to her parents as Supreme Beings that provide everything for her. As she deepens her relationship with her parents, she begins to become aware that there may be other powers in the world, but her first relationship is with her parents. As soon as she goes to school and encounters teachers and mentors, she begins to develop other relationships that allow her to grow, but the formative years are about the child's relationship with parents, teachers, and mentors (including aunts, uncles, and other adults she interacts with). Ruth is the deeper understanding of this relationship, and the experience of God in that relationship with a parent or mentor.

As a baby becomes a toddler and a young child, he starts to experience the gamut of all feelings. He may or may not know how to manage his feelings, but as he grows in his independence and explores the world, he is confronted with all sorts of emotions. King David's book of Psalms is the spiritual reflection of that experience. Psalms helps us integrate all the emotions of humanity and see God's presence in each one. Like the toddler who is scared or grateful, Psalms guides us to experience God in each of these feelings.

The existential angst of a teenager can be expressed in two simple words that he or she often exclaims: Why me? The travails of love and growth, school and family, combine inside a teenager into the feeling of suffering (or persecution, depending on the teenager's integration of the feelings). These feelings are common, sadly resulting in suicides being the third leading cause of death for children, teens, and young adults ages ten to twenty-four.[1] The feeling of suffering, like Job, is intense and powerful. Mirrored decades later by many people going through a midlife crisis of the spiritual nature, the book of Job guides us to integrate the suffering into an awareness of the Divine.

The rest of the books are all reflective of the journeys that all people go through in different cycles throughout their adult lives. Depending on how they interact with their surroundings, all people will go through experiences within their communities or jobs (Proverbs); all different aspects of Life, especially as their elders die (Ecclesiastes); passion and sexuality (Song of Songs); and real pain and loss due to their own actions (Lamentations). As people get older, they start to become more cognizant of time itself (Daniel), hopefully having moments "in the zone" as well as an appreciation for both time and timelessness. Time is an adult "issue," as is both the "absence of God" and excessive/addictive behavior (Esther). Few adults don't know someone who has had an addiction problem, and most people of at least middle age have experienced the death of someone as a direct or indirect result of that addictive behavior. Whether it is because of inspiration or desperation, most adults make a conscious choice to take responsibility for their lives through work (Ezra-Nehemiah-Chronicles). There comes a point in people's lives when they realize that there is deep reward in seeing the fruits of their labors and, like Ezra-Nehemiah, they choose to work hard toward specific goals.

Viewed as a model for the spiritual journey into experiencing God in every relationship, the typical person's process of psychological development is the perfect order for these sacred texts. In the same way that each human being grows internally as he or she ages (and hopefully matures), the books that we have explored are guides to helping each of us recognize the Divinity in all experiences. Ketuvim is the prescription needed for the healing and growth into personal spiritual maturity.

More important than the sequence, however, is the content. The books beg us to answer the questions, Are we really ready to begin to experience God in each moment, in every relationship, and in every place? Do we have the courage to go down that path of awakening to the Divinity in everything?

Each book contains a myriad of great lessons, and each book gives us tools to enhance, deepen, and bring wholeness to any experience that we have in life. It could be a lifetime's work to truly explore any one of these great books in depth. To be honestly aware of God in the midst of our suffering (Job), our passion (Song of Songs), or any other relationship discussed could take decades of conscious practice. Each one of these sacred Writings teaches an entire discipline in and of itself. But what would happen if each of us decided to really explore not just one of the books but all of them? How would we act if we really understood the teachings inside all these books together? What would we need to do?

"With great power comes great responsibility."

Although quoted by everyone from Franklin Roosevelt to Winston Churchill to Spider-Man's Uncle Ben, the words of Voltaire come alive if we interpret them only slightly differently: with greater awareness of the Divine in each moment comes great responsibility.

As we begin to experience God in every relationship in our lives, which is the underlying theme and goal of these sacred texts of Ketuvim, then, like Ezra and Nehemiah, we have little choice but to act on that awareness. Those of us who have ever had an epiphany of any sort know that the experience changes who we are. Although our awareness as the result of that numinous encounter is enhanced and enlarged, our choices of behavior become more limited as it becomes increasingly difficult to act in opposition to the lessons of the experience.

On a simplistic level, if we truly understand the violation and loss that is involved as a result of theft, it becomes nearly impossible to take even a hand towel or hanger from a hotel that we stay in. If we know the depths of pain that come about when a partner violates a relationship with us, it becomes difficult to get involved with someone who is in a monogamous relationship with another. Spiritual awareness is no different in its process.

Once a person experiences the Divine in a relationship, it affects forever how he or she chooses to interact in parallel circumstances. With self-awareness comes self-responsibility. Experiencing God in a relationship with pain, as we learn from Lamentations, guides us to choosing different behavior so as not to have that pain again. No longer can we choose to rationalize or ignore things in the same way that we did prior to the understanding, nor can we blame another and deny our own responsibility. Similarly each book of Ketuvim teaches us how to experience God in circumstances and relationships in such a way that our daily behavior changes. Herein lies the deep power in these texts.

These sacred Writings are significantly different than any other part of the Bible. While both the Torah and the Prophets sections of the Bible give teachings and laws, and demand ethical behavior through different methods, the Writings encourage that ethical behavior by taking readers on a personal journey through their own life experiences in such a way as to find God in every place. The texts are less "preaching and teaching" than they are "awakening to the experience." With that awakening comes a shift in behavior. These Writings are not meant just to teach us, but to move through and change us. If we allow the words to really come inside us and help us experience God in each type of relationship that we have in life, then our very essence shifts into a more aware, joyous, conscious, and ethical way of being.

Looked at this way, the books are clearly tied together. Each helps us in a single aspect of our lives, and collectively they have the potential of guiding us into the realization that every moment is holy, every experience sacred, every place Divine. As we each have that realization at deeper and deeper levels, then it becomes that much easier for each of us to truly manifest our *tikkun HaOlam*, our distinctive piece of repairing the world that only we can do.

That unique piece that is exclusively each individual's is exactly what Ketuvim can awaken, teach, and guide a person into creating. Ketuvim, if read with conscious intention, can help all people find themselves, their souls, and their purpose in life in the deepest of ways through the experience of God in every relationship. It is as if each of us has a specific note to play on a special instrument in the symphony of Life. Using Ketuvim to know God in each relationship that we have allows us to find our instrument and play that note. When each of us does just that, it is truly the sound of heaven on earth.

May we let the sacred Writings open up our hearts and souls to be able to experience God in every moment, in every hour, and in every place. May we be blessed to take that experience and share it with others so that all of Life sings in harmony and joy. And may we be blessed to have our faces lifted, and to know peace.

Thank you for kindly letting me be a part of your journey in Life through these sacred texts.

Note

1. "Ten Leading Causes of Death and Injury," 2010, Centers for Disease Control and Prevention, http://www.cdc.gov/injury/wisqars/Leading Causes.html.

Glossary

Aish HaTorah: International Orthodox Jewish school, outreach program, and adult educational organization

Aramaic: Ancient language similar to Hebrew that was the spoken language in the time of the second temple

Bamidbar Rabbah: Twelfth-century commentary on the book of Numbers

Bava Batra: "The Last Gate"; a Talmudic tractate that deals extensively with tort law

BCE: Before the Common Era, equivalent in date to BC

Berachot: "Blessings"; a Talmudic tractate that deals extensively with blessings and prayer

Bereshit Rabbah: A homiletic commentary on the book of Genesis from the second to third centuries

CE: Common Era, equivalent in date to AD

Cyrus: Persian king of the sixth century BCE

Eruvin: "Mixtures"; a Talmudic tractate that deals extensively with the Sabbath and the traveling laws surrounding it

Eshet Chayil: "Woman of Valor"; the name given to the last chapter of the book of Proverbs

Gemara: Commentary on the Mishnah of Judah HaNasi; codified by the sixth century CE; one of the two main components of the Talmud, along with the Mishnah

gematria: Practice of equating Hebrew letters with numerical values, and understanding hidden meanings of words and phrases as a result

Great Assembly: Also known as the Sanhedrin, it was the Supreme Court of biblical Israel, comprised of seventy-one judges

Ibn Ezra: Rabbi Abraham Ibn Ezra, 1089–1164; Spanish rabbinic commentator

Jonathan ben Uzziel: First-century-CE Talmudic sage; author of Targum Yonatan, an Aramaic commentary on Nevi'im

Kabbalah: Jewish mysticism, from the root *Kabal*, meaning "to receive"

Kabir: 1440–1518, Indian poet, mystic, and saint

Kahlil Gibran: 1883–1931, Lebanese-American poet; the third best-selling poet of all time behind Shakespeare and Lao-tzu

Ketuvim: "Writings"; the third section of the Hebrew Bible

Kundalini: In yoga, the coiled, passionate, and unconscious energy of creativity and sexuality

Likutey Mohoran: The main work of Rebbe Nachman of Breslov, including his philosophies and teachings of spirituality and mysticism

Liturgy of the Hours: *Liturgia Horarum*, the Catholic Church's official set of daily prayers to be recited at specific times throughout the day

Makkot: "Lashes"; a Talmudic tractate that deals extensively with laws and punishment

Megillah: "Scroll"; a Talmudic tractate that deals with public Torah reading and the practices of the holiday Purim

Midrash: A homiletic approach to understanding text at a deeper level using stories and oral tradition

Midrash Mishlei: A Midrashic text from the eleventh century focusing on understanding the book of Proverbs

Midrash Shmuel: A Midrashic text from the eleventh century focusing on understanding the books of Samuel

Midrash Tehillim: A Midrashic text from the eleventh century focusing on understanding the book of Psalms

Mishnah: "Secondary"; first written version of the Oral Law given to Moses on Mount Sinai; redacted by Rabbi Judah HaNasi in the third century CE

Mishnah Yadayim: "Mishnah of the hands"; a Mishnaic tractate that deals extensively with rabbinic impurities

Moab: A neighboring nation of ancient Israel located in current Jordan

Napoleon Hill: 1883–1970, author, philosopher, and advisor to President Franklin Roosevelt; author of the business classic *Think and Grow Rich* (1937)

Ner Tamid: The Eternal Light; always lit in the ancient temple as well as in all synagogues

Nevi'im: "Prophets"; the second section of the Hebrew Bible

Ohr Hachaim HaKodosh: "The Sacred Light of the Holy"; eighteenth-century commentary on the Torah written by the sage of the same name

Passover: Jewish festival commemorating the exodus from Egypt

Pirkei Avot: "Ethics of Our Fathers"; Mishnaic tractate that deals extensively with appropriate ethical behavior between people; the only tractate that deals exclusively with ethical behavior and morals rather than laws

Pirkei de-Rabbi Eliezer: "Ethics of Rabbi Eliezer"; ethical commentary authored by R. Eliezer ben Hyrcanus in the first/second centuries

Purim: Jewish holiday in the spring commemorating the saving of the Jews from persecution as told in the book of Esther

Rabbi Akiva: Akiva ben Joseph; first- and second-century Talmudic rabbi considered one of the greatest legalists and mystics in Jewish history; the spiritual leader of the Bar Kochba Rebellion

Rabbi Eleazar: Eleazar ben Hycanus; first- and second-century Talmudic rabbi attributed with mystical powers; the teacher of Rabbi Akiva

Rabbi Gamaliel: First- and second-century Talmudic rabbi; the first to lead the Sanhedrin after the destruction of the temple and the fall of Jerusalem

Rabbi Hiyya bar Abba: second- and third-century Talmudic rabbi; legalist who focused on ethical behavior

Rabbi Joshua: Joshua ben Hananiah; first- and second-century Talmudic rabbi known for his expressions of wisdom in subtle but clever ways

Rabbi Judah HaNasi: "Judah the Prince"; second-century redactor and editor of the Mishnah

Rabbi Shimon Schwab: 1908–95, one of the leading Orthodox rabbis in Germany and America; known for combining wisdom from both secular and highly religious worlds into accessible teachings for the twentieth century

Rabbi Yochanan ben Zakkai: First-century Talmudic rabbi and leader of the Academy at Yavneh

Ramban: 1194–1270, Rabbi Moshe ben Nachman (aka Nachmanides); Kabbalist; argued against the Catholic Church in the 1263 Disputations of Barcelona

Rashi: 1040–1105, Rabbi Shlomo Yitzak; French commentator on Talmud and Tanakh

Rav Hamnuna: Third-century Talmudic rabbi; became the head of the Academy at Sura

Rebbe Nachman: 1772–1810, great grandson of the Baal Shem Tov; founder of the Breslov Hasidic Movement; mystic who taught through storytelling and song

Robert Bly: Best-selling author of *Iron John* (1990); university professor; poet

Ruach HaKodesh: "Holy Spirit"; the masculine aspect of God in the physical world

Rumi: 1207–73, Jalal al-Din Muhammed Rumi; mystic poet of the Sufi tradition of Islam; author of the *Mathnawi*; in 2007 recognized as the most popular poet in America

Sanhedrin: The Great Assembly; the Supreme Court of biblical Israel comprised of seventy-one judges

Seder Olam Rabbah: "The Great Order of the World"; second-century Hebraic text that details the dates from creation to Alexander's conquest of Persia; attributed to Yose ben Halafta

Sefer Yetzirah: "Book of Formation"; mystical text attributed to Abraham and redacted by Rabbi Akiva

Shabbat: "Sabbath"; a Talmudic tractate that deals extensively with the practices required on the Sabbath

Shavuot: Jewish festival of "Weeks" (it occurs seven weeks after Passover) that commemorates the giving of Torah on Mount Sinai

Shekhinah: The female aspect of God in the physical world

Shir HaShirim Rabbah: Eighth-century commentary on Song of Songs

Solomon Ibn Gabirol: 1021–58, Jewish mystical poet and philosopher from Andalusia

Sotah: "Adulterous Wife"; a Talmudic tractate that deals extensively with the issues around adultery and punishment

Succah: "Booth"; a Talmudic tractate that deals extensively with the laws and customs regarding the celebration of the Jewish festival of Sukkot

Sukkot: "Booths"; Jewish festival commemorating the wandering of the Hebrews through the desert; participants dwell in temporary structures for the duration of the holiday

Talmud: "Instruct" and "study"; the "Oral Torah" comprised of the Mishnah and the Gemara; includes laws and lore and is the basis of Jewish practices in modern times

Tanakh: The Hebrew Bible; an acronym for Torah, Neviʾim, Ketuvim

Targum: A translation and interpretation of a section of the Hebrew Bible composed between the destruction of the temple and the Middle Ages

Targum Jonathan ben Uzziel: The Talmudic commentary on Neviʾim

Targum Onkelos: The Talmudic commentary on Torah

Teilhard de Chardin: 1881–1955, French philosopher, poet, and Jesuit priest

teshuvah: "Return" or "reconciliation"; the process required for fixing errors against others *tikkun HaOlam*: "Repair of the World"; an understanding that everyone has one's own piece of the world to repair, and the responsibility to cause healing where there is hurt in the world

Tisha B'Av: The ninth day of the Hebrew month of Av; the most tragic day in Jewish history

Torah: The first five books of the Hebrew Bible

Tree of Life: A model of the universe as symbolized by the Torah

Yah: A name for God; the first two letters of the tetragrammaton

YHWH: The tetragrammaton; the four-lettered name of God used in the Hebrew Bible

Yogi Bhajan Khalsa: 1929–2004, Indian guru who introduced America to the yogic practice of Kundalini Yoga; the leader of the Sikh religion in North America

Yoma: "Day"; a Talmudic tractate that deals extensively with the laws and practices surrounding the Jewish holiday of Yom Kippur

Zohar: "Splendor"; Jewish mystical text that is the basis for much of Kabbalah; traditionally attributed to the Talmudic Rabbi Shimon bar Yohai; modernly attributed to Rabbi Moshe de Leon (Spain, 1250–1305)